Enneagram 2 manuscripts in 1

A Self Awareness and Personal Growth Journey to Understanding Yourself and Find Your Personality Type

Written By Beto Canales & Habits of Wisdom

© **Copyright 2019 Beto Canales & Habits of Wisdom - All rights reserved.**

The content contained within this book may not be reproduced, duplicated or transmitted without direct written permission from the author or the publisher.

Under no circumstances will any blame or legal responsibility be held against the publisher, or author, for any damages, reparation, or monetary loss due to the information contained within this book. Either directly or indirectly.

Legal Notice:

This book is copyright protected. This book is only for personal use. You cannot amend, distribute, sell, use, quote or paraphrase any part, or the content within this book, without the consent of the author or publisher.

Disclaimer Notice:

Please note the information contained within this document is for educational and entertainment purposes only. All effort has been executed to present accurate, up to date, and reliable, complete information. No warranties of any kind are declared or implied. Readers acknowledge that the author is not engaging in the rendering of legal, financial, medical or professional advice. The content within this book has been derived from various sources. Please consult a licensed professional before attempting any techniques outlined in this book.

By reading this document, the reader agrees that under no circumstances is the author responsible for any losses, direct or indirect, which are incurred as a result of the use of information contained within this document, including, but not limited to, — errors, omissions, or inaccuracies.

Table of Contents

Book - I

Introduction..11

Chapter 1: The History Of The Enneagram......................13

    The History Of Óscar Ichazo..............................14

    The History of Claudio Benjamín Naranjo Cohen........15

Chapter 2: Why The Enneagram Is Relevant To Everyone 19

    The Overview Of The Nine Personality Types..............22

    The Wings And The Centers Of The Enneagram Structure..24

Chapter 3: Type One - The Perfectionist..........................26

    Ones In The Workplace..29

    Ones And Relationships..32

Chapter 4: Type Two - The Helper..................................36

    Twos In The Workplace 40

    Twos And Their Relationships......................................44

Chapter 5: Type 3 - The Performer 46

Threes In The Workplace 51

Threes And Relationships 54

Chapter 6: Type 4- The Romantic 57

Fours In The Workplace 61

Fours And Relationships 65

Chapter 7: Type 5 - The Investigator 68

Fives In The Workplace 72

Fives And Relationships 75

Chapter 8: Type 6 - The Loyalist 79

Sixes In The Workplace 83

Sixes In Relationships 86

Chapter 9: Type 7 - The Enthusiast 89

Sevens In The Workplace 94

Sevens In Relationships 96

Chapter 10: Type 8 - The Challenger 99

Eights In The Workplace 103

Eights In Relationships 106

Chapter 11: Type 9 - The Peacemaker 109

Nines In The Workplace 113

Nines In Relationships	117
Chapter 12: The Enneagram Wings	119
Type One To Type Four And Their Wings	121
Type Five To Type Nine And Their Wings	124
Chapter 13: Introduction To Centers	132
The Instinctive Center	133
The Feeling Center	136
The Thinking Center	138
Bonus Chapter: Enneagram in Relationships	142
Using the Enneagram in Your Relationship	142
Why Use the Enneagram in Your Relationship?	143
Areas of Your Relationship in Which the Enneagram Can Help	146
Spiritual Relationships with the Enneagram	148
Conclusion	150
The Enneagram Test Where You Can Discover Your Personality	156
Your Personality Type Can Be Found Right Here	167
References	170

Book - II

Introduction	172

Chapter 1 : Enneagram, Its Origins and Types 176

   How to Use the Enneagram 179

      Benefits of the Enneagram 181

      Quick Overview of the Types and Triads 184

Chapter 2 : Enneagram Test 188

   The Test 189

Chapter 3 : The Types 203

Chapter 4 : Enneagram as a Self-Discovery and Introspection Tool 214

   Enneagram for Self-Improvement and Introspection 217

   5 Exercises for Self-discovery Using the Enneagram 224

Chapter 5 : Using the Enneagram in Your Relationship 227

   Why Use the Enneagram in Your Relationship? 228

   Areas of Your Relationship in Which the Enneagram Can Help 232

   Spiritual Relationships with the Enneagram 234

Chapter 6 : The Personality Types in Relationships 237

   Types in Relationships 237

Chapter 7 : 7 Key Areas that Control Your Partner's Behavior 250

   Real Life Key Areas 255

Chapter 8 : 7 Tips for Bringing the Best Out in Each Other 260

Real Life Potential 267
Compliment-a-Day Exercise 271

Chapter 9 : Improving Communication in Your Relationship 273

16 Activities to Foster Satisfaction and Effective Communication 275
Find What Works for You 283

Chapter 10 : Common Misconceptions and Frequently Asked Questions 284

Frequently Asked Questions about the Enneagram .. 288
Real Life Problems Starting 289

Chapter 11 : Write it Out 293

Writing in Your Relationship 294
7 Writing Activities 297

Chapter 12 : Enneagram in All Your Relationships 301

The Enneagram at Work 302
Your Friends and Family 303
Real Life Family Enneagram 306

Bonus Chapter: "Enneagram Self Discovery" 314

The Enneagram Wings 314

- Type One To Type Four And Their Wings 316
- Type Five To Type Nine And Their Wings 319
- Bonus Chapter: "Enneagram Self Discovery" 327
  - Introduction To Centers 327
  - The Instinctive Center 328
  - The Feeling Center 331
  - The Thinking Center 333
- Conclusion 337
- References 340

Book - I

Enneagram Self Discovery

A Self Awareness and Personal Growth Journey to Understanding Yourself and Find Your Personality Type

Introduction

You probably have not put a lot of thought into your personality, and its type, however, it is highly important for everyone to know their personality types. That is because if they knew their personality types and everything that there is to know about themselves, it would greatly influence them on going into areas of their lives that best suits them.

With that said, if people understood their personality types, they would only go into careers that best suits them. Additionally, this would also influence them on whether or not they should settle down, get married, or even have kids. Or, if they do choose to get married based on their personality type, they would be pickier as far as who to hook up with based on knowing whether he or she would be the right fit. This would lead to fewer divorces and many more happy marriages as opposed to being married out of convenience.

In other words, if people knew more about their personality types, then they would be happier in general, they would be at peace, and simply be more comfortable in their own skin. They could also become the best versions of themselves which would bring them the ultimate happiness. And that means they would be able to once and for all banish confusion, and the good news is that they can! You are now wondering how can people possibly know what personality type they have?

They would do that by becoming familiar with the Enneagram which is a tool that is extremely powerful when it comes to learning about who you are and using it to transform you in incredible ways!

Before going into the nitty gritty of the Enneagram, you will need to know about the history of it in order to understand its origin and purpose. This will be discussed in the first chapter.

Chapter 1: The History Of The Enneagram

This may be the first time you have ever heard of the term Enneagram, or if not, you likely don't know much about it. And, in this chapter, the history of the Enneagram will be covered. The references are derived from the 1994 paperback *The Enneagram Made Easy: Discover the 9 Types of People* which was written by the late author, Elizabeth Wagele, and therapist Renee Baron.

The history of the Enneagram is still quite unknown. However, the origin of the word Enneagram is derived from the Greek, *enna* which means nine, and *gramma* which means something that is drawn or written. With that said, the Enneagram is also referred to as the Enneagram Of Personality. What it is, presents the human psyche and the 9 personality types or they are referred to as the enneatypes.

The origin of this model comes from over a century ago, and it has influences from the late Russian mystic and philosopher, George Ivanovich Gurdjieff. However, it is unknown whether the emergence of the Enneagram came from the Chilean-born psychologist, Claudio Benjamín Naranjo Cohen, or the Bolivian-born psychologist, Óscar

Ichazo. However, both of these psychologists from South America had used the Enneagram Of Personality in their teachings. And both psychologists were founders and pioneers of important aspects of psychology.

However, since it the Enneagram derived from the teachings of possibly both psychologists, you will want to know about the history of Óscar Ichazo and Claudio Benjamín Naranjo Cohen, and what their roles were. The history of Óscar Ichazo will be covered in the following section of this chapter.

The History Of Óscar Ichazo

Óscar Ichazo was born in July 1931 in Bolivia, and he was the founder of the Arica School in 1968 which was named after Arica, Chile where he once lived. This school is a human potential movement group has anyone who had studied at this institute will have learned methods on how to raise cosmic consciousness. And, according to his that was written in 1982, *Interviews With Oscar Ichazo*, he became interested in psychology in 1954 as he started to study the behavior and thought pattern repeating itself. And then he discovered along the way there are 9 ways that an individual's ego will settle within the psyche during the first years of childhood.

And the more he studied this phenomenon, he had found connections between the 9 different personalities and mapped out the circle, the lines, and the points. This is how the Enneagram came to be which he had used in his teachings when he had founded the Arica School in 1968. However, again, it is unknown if Ichazo had established the Enneagram, or if it was Claudio Benjamín Naranjo Cohen who had. In the final section of this chapter, more about Claudio Benjamín Naranjo Cohen will be covered.

The History of Claudio Benjamín Naranjo Cohen

Claudio Benjamín Naranjo Cohen or Claudio Naranjo was born in November 1932 and was a Chilean-born psychologist. He was considered the first to combine both spiritual as well as psychology into one, and he also founded the Seekers After Truth Institute, and he may have been the one to establish the Enneagram. His take on psychology was unique as he had incorporated spirituality with psychotherapy, and his way of teaching psychology and therapy methods were unique. In fact, the German-born psychologist Fritz Perls who founded Gestalt Therapy had named Claudio Naranjo as one of his 3 successors.

And, after years and years of studying psychology and spirituality, he had believed to have established the Enneagram which he had mentioned in his book from 1991, *Character and Neurosis: An Integrative View*. He had been extremely active in his studies and in his practice while he traveled all over the world to teach his findings and teach the principles of the Enneagram which is how he had become a renowned psychologist.

With that said, it is possible that both Claudio Naranjo and Oscar Ichazo had established the Enneagram because they are psychologists that have a unique way of studying the psyche. However, the likely reason that Ichazo was not said to be the one who had established this model is that some newer Enneagram of Personality writers had stated that he had published factual ideas which could not be copyrighted because of the fact that they were factual, he did not establish those theories.

Either way, regardless of which psychologist had established the Enneagram indicated that both have had a unique way of studying and analyzing the psyche because the Enneagram is essential for people to understand what they can about themselves.

As it was previously mentioned, the Enneagram model is there to help people in their business, personal, and in any aspect of their lives in general so that they receive a better understanding of themselves. And, before the age of Claudio Naranjo and Oscar Ichazo's work, this phenomenon was not considered because it was not known until both of these psychologists had started using its principles and using it in their teachings.

And, once the Enneagram is understood, and utilized by people, it will help them direct themselves towards the line of work they are the most suitable for, as well as the personality type of friends that they can make and maintain. And, this will help them attract the most suitable mate that has the personality type that would be well suited for them.

The Enneagram would help people avoid situations that could lead them to failure and heartache which would have been a result of their doing by getting into situations that would not fit their personality type. On the other hand, sometimes people do need to experience failure and heartache regardless of the situation in order to evolve and to grow.

With that said, in the next chapter, you will learn about the details about the Enneagram before each of the 9 personality types are covered. And the references for these details are derived from *The Enneagram Made Easy:*

Discover the 9 Types of People, written by the late author, Elizabeth Wagele, and therapist Renee Baron; as well as from *Personality Types: Using the Enneagram for Self-Discovery* that was written by Don Richard Riso who was an American teacher of the Enneagram of Personality and had formed the Enneagram Institute in 1997.

Chapter 2: Why The Enneagram Is Relevant To Everyone

The Enneagram is the most powerful tool for people to understand who they are as the late Don Richard Riso had stated in his books, including his paperback, *Personality Types: Using the Enneagram for Self-Discovery*. It has already been covered that the Enneagram represents 9 different personalities and archetypes which is meant to help people understand who they are, and why they act, think, and feel in relation to others, the world, and most importantly- themselves.

And, you may be thinking that the Enneagram represents those silly personality quizzes that you are told to take online to find out what personality matches your type. However, even though there may be a slight element of truth to that, what the Enneagram represents more than your personality type is that it delves quite deep into your fears, your strong motivations, and defense mechanisms. And these factors are what make up your personality as it is found buried deep underneath the structure of each personality.

Studies at Iowa State University have shown that there are positive effects of Enneagram on the well-being in a psychological way. Additionally, other studies have revealed that once young adults are aware of the effects of the Enneagram, they have an easier time accepting themselves.

Let's use the analogy of the onion and compare it to how the Enneagram picks apart your personality. The outer layer of the onion is what represents your general personality, and it is smooth. It is just the surface, and not much can be seen beyond that. However, once you start peeling that onion, then you start to see underneath the surface as the layers of the onion are removed. You see that it is not nearly as smooth as you dig deeper, and the smell of the onion is strong, and it can make you cry. The Enneagram does the same to your personality, the outer layer of it. Once it is picked apart and layers are removed, then the core motivations, the deep-rooted fears, and the reason behind the defense mechanisms are found.

With that said, people learning their own personality type without peeling the outer layer will not learn much from it. Just like the surface layer of the onion does not add much flavor to your cooking. However, once each layer is removed, then people will learn a lot about why they are the way they are - and they can learn about how they relate to others and the world, as well as themselves. It will be uncomfortable to learn what makes up any personality, but in the end, it is quite helpful and healing. Just like how it is rough cutting an onion and removing the layers. The smell is strong, and it makes you cry. But once the inner parts of the onion are added to the meal that you are cooking, it provides the meal with a fantastic flavor.

And, people who have learned to use the Enneagram for their benefit, they have in many ways healed and become at peace within themselves. They find out why they behave the way they do; they find out why they have the particular tastes that they have, and why they are repelled by certain things. And that doesn't mean that they have to fight their urges to be repelled by certain stimuli unless they want to heal from a particular phobia. In fact, they shouldn't do that, as that would go against their nature.

And, in order to fully understand the structure of the Enneagram, you will learn about the 9 personalities, as well as its wings and the center. In the next sections of this chapter, a brief overview of the personalities, the wings, and its centers will be covered before getting into the nitty-gritty of each one. The first thing to be covered is a brief overview of the 9 personalities.

The Overview Of The Nine Personality Types

Here is the part you have been looking forward to about the Enneagram, as you will learn about the personality types that are part of its structure. The 9 personality types are:

- **Type One - The Perfectionist** - This type is known to have the need to get it right all the time, wants to keep improving everything, and is the responsible type.

- **Type Two - The Helper** - This type is the one that wants to help everyone and wants to always be the one that is needed in every situation.

- **Type Three - The Performer** - This type is the one who always wants to achieve something great and has to be successful because that is what validates this type.

- **Type Four - The Romantic** - This type is the one that believes that love can be regained from any failed situation or relationship and had an idealistic mindset. And this type is incredibly empathetic.

- **Type Five - The Investigator** - This type is

always the type to observe, study, and keep to themselves.

- **Type Six - The Loyalist** - This type has a difficult time trusting others and wants to trust but struggles to do so on a constant basis.

- **Type Seven - The Enthusiast** - This type is always looking for fun and adventure and are always looking forward to something in the future.

- **Type Eight - The Challenger** - This type is the one that has to be in control and is always up for a challenge. They are quite strong-willed and will never accept defeat.

- **Type Nine - The Peacemaker** - This type is always looking for peace and harmony and do what they can to avoid conflict at all costs.

Those are the 9 personalities that make up the Enneagram structure. There is a good chance that you have spotted several of these personalities that fit you the best. With that said, you may be thinking that several of these descriptions fit you the best, and not just one. That is why the Enneagram structure comes with wings and the centers which will be briefly discussed in the last section of this chapter.

The Wings And The Centers Of The Enneagram Structure

The wings of the Enneagram as it is referenced in late Riso's book, *Personality Types: Using the Enneagram for Self-Discovery* are the 2 types that are adjacent to your main type in the model. In other words, you can think of them as close neighbors that influence you but are not strong enough to have a huge impact on your core.

In order to help you understand this better, think about getting an ice cream sundae. The flavor of the sundae will be vanilla, which is your core. But you will want to add something else to make the sundae flavored even more by adding fudge, caramel, and some sprinkles. The fudge, caramel, and the sprinkles will influence the flavor, but the main flavor will always be vanilla. That is what the wings of the Enneagram represent. They influence your core but don't change it. The wings are there to help people understand more about their core type, as well as how they relate to others and the world around them. And you can say as well that the wings are there to help balance the core.

The wings can help you problem-solve and gain a better

understanding of life in general. That is what helps people stay balanced, just like an airplane that needs its wings to keep their core balanced while it is in the air. And, in addition to the wings, the Enneagram model also consists of 3 centers which are the negative aspects of any personality. The 3 centers are:

- **The Instinctive Center** as 3 personality types fall into this area and this area represents rage and anger
- **The Feeling Center** as 3 personality types also fall into this center and this area represents shame
- **The Thinking Center** as 3 personality types falls into this area as well, and this center represents fear.

And the personalities of the types that fall into the center are impacted by its emotional nature. However, more about the wings and the centers will be discussed later on in this eBook. The first thing that will be covered in the chapters to come are the 9 personality types of the Enneagram. And, the first personality that will be covered in the following chapter is Type One - The Perfectionist.

Chapter 3: Type One - The Perfectionist

The Type One or Perfectionist personality type is the first to be covered as the description of this personality is quite self-explanatory. As it is referred to in the late Riso's book, *Personality Types: Using the Enneagram for Self-Discovery*, those individuals who match this personality as they will be referred to as One's are never happy until things are perfect in their eyes.

Ones will never accept any flaws from themselves, and from others, and from any situation. They are always stressing about how to constantly improve anything that they encounter. Their way of thinking is idealistic whenever it comes to putting chaos in order which they cannot accept that it rarely can be done. Or if it can be done, it will not happen in a timely manner. And even though it is always admirable to have the desire to keep improving and becoming the best versions of oneself, the Ones take it to the extreme. They take it to the level that is clearly unattainable.

Each time they find that a goal they have made for themselves is unattainable, then they become guilty that they failed as failure is not an option for Ones. And when they are guilty, they become angry, and then they become guilty of being angry. This guilt and anger cycle becomes a vicious one, and this is a cycle that cannot be broken by the Perfectionist type.

It is clear that no one is harder on them other than themselves. If they get something wrong or if they miss points for anything they work hard to do, then they will berate themselves for not being good enough. They cannot handle just not getting it 'right' whatever it may be. They have a very difficult time relaxing and don't understand how to enjoy the small pleasures in life. They are too anxious, stressed, and too occupied with the ideas of perfection in every situation in order to find joy, and they almost never laugh either.

One's personality type would have emerged in early childhood. Even as early as a year old when they stumbled while learning to walk. They would have gotten very upset over tumbling over other toddlers that are of other personality types. And as they had matured and grown, while they gained more awareness, their perfectionist style became more prominent when they started going to school.

If they had difficulty with reading or doing a math problem, they would not be able to accept that they were struggling. They would have been the types to call themselves stupid and other names, which in the end would have been damaging to their self-esteem. That also meant that these types would have been upset over getting a 99 percent mark on a test or an assignment because it did not reach that 100 mark. Other personality types would have been thrilled to have gotten a high mark; they would have been thrilled to have aced the test or the assignment. But not the Ones.

The same applied whenever it came to friendships. Especially if they wanted to become friends or even develop a relationship with someone who they were fond of and were turned down. They would ruminate about what they could have done to repel the individual that they were fond of and would then berate themselves for not being perfect, and likable. They could never understand that sometimes a lack of chemistry is the reason that friendships and relationships don't work out. They take full responsibility for it.

However, the positive traits the Ones are known to have is that they are responsible, organized, hard-working, and are list-makers, and very loyal. They also follow the rules carefully and expect others to follow the rules as well. This now brings this to covering how Ones behave in the workplace as well as the type of occupations that are the most fitting for this personality type. In the next section of this chapter, the way Ones are in the workplace will be covered.

Ones In The Workplace

According to what is written about the Ones in the workplace based on what is written in the late Riso's book, *Personality Types: Using the Enneagram for Self-Discovery*, there is no doubt at all based on the serious nature that they take their jobs seriously. In fact, Ones are known to be workaholics and will refuse to go back home until all of their tasks at work are completed - perfectly. And they will come back home being anxious about whether or not they had done a good job with their work as they would be nervous about how the boss will respond to their efforts - and they will constantly think about the feedback.

In fact, they will keep worrying about the boss' feedback about their performance at work is less than perfect and this will literally keep them up at night. That also means that because they are extremely serious and have an incredible amount of self-control and self-discipline when it comes to their work and anything else they do in their lives, they are naturally industrious, take the rules seriously, they are practical, they are organized and are the ideal employee for any company to have. That is because the Ones are guaranteed to do a fantastic job, regardless of how they feel about it which will likely be not good enough since that is within their nature to not take pride in any work they do. That is clearly because it is far from perfect.

However, even though they are the ideal employee for any company, type Ones would only thrive in these particular types of jobs which are:

- Financial Planning
- Banking
- Blogging
- Writing
- Property Management
- Any Manager
- Attorney
- Accountant
- Professor

- Scientist

- Technician

- Welder

- Artist

- Any Type of CEO

As much as the Ones are natural born followers when it comes to the rules, they are also natural-born leaders. However, only a few personality types would be able to work under the Perfectionist manager. Other Ones would clash with them terribly. And, Ones would make excellent managers as far as making sure that the employees that they are managing get the work done perfectly and in a timely manner.

That also makes you wonder how Ones would be able to manage relationships of any kind since they not only expect perfection from themselves but expect it from others. That is considering that they would put a lot of pressure on anyone who they end up having any kind of relationship with. That means anyone who they are in a personal relationship with, or friends, or co-workers. Before that is looked into, the types of jobs that the Ones are not ideal for will give you an idea of how their personal relationships would be. The types of jobs that the Ones are better off avoiding are:

- Teaching Kindergarten or elementary school-aged children

- Comedy Improv

- Doctors

- Nursing

- Bartending

- Waiting

- Or any job that requires them to deal with people on a regular basis except for those they work with.

That is why the Ones make good managers and CEOs. And in the last section of this chapter, the types of relationships they end up with, as well as the struggles will be covered.

Ones And Relationships

Because of the fact that Ones expect as much perfection out of others as much as they do of themselves, they would have a difficult time maintaining relationships. And many of them end up in divorce for these traits as well. That is because they are not compassionate and expect their partners to follow the rules and they always put them high up on a pedestal which they always fall from in the end. That is when the relationships with the Ones become sour. That goes for marriage, dating, friendships, and any relationships that they would form with co-workers.

In fact, many of the One's co-workers would not want to work with them because they would feel uncomfortable and bullied by them since they will be judged harshly. And, many of the co-workers would do what they can to avoid them. However, other co-workers that are Ones would clash and would even get into heated arguments.

Even though the Ones appear that they are the types that would not able to have a relationship with anyone because of their judgmental and highly analytical nature, there are personality types that would be able to maintain a relationship with the Ones. More information on that will be covered later on in this eBook. That is because even though Ones expect perfection and are very hard on those who they are in relationships with, they are still extremely loyal, take their relationships seriously, and are extremely honest which are traits that are extremely desirable and respectable.

However, Ones can make difficult parents as well as they would put a lot of expectations on their kids and could unintentionally cause their kids to have anxiety about getting things done correctly. Their kids at school would be afraid to show them a test that they had failed or did not do well on because of knowing that their Type One parent would react angrily towards them. They would also fall into the authoritarian parenting style which means they control every aspect of their children's lives. That will only cause their children to have low self-esteem or become rebellious and not want to have anything to do with their Type One as they become older and more independent.

Many Type One Parents would also not be able to accept a child with special needs because of the fact that in their eyes, a child with a disability would be less than perfect. However, there would be some Type One parents that would accept the child with a disability if they saw the potential for the child to do well later on and would work tirelessly with them to help them get to that point.

To sum up about the Type One - Perfectionist, those who have this personality type are what their type is labeled as which has a perfectionist way of thinking. They expect themselves to be perfect and are constantly improving themselves to the point of obsession. They also expect the same from others whether it is their mates, their peer, their friends, their co-workers, and kids. Yet at the same time, they are also quite loyal, honest, dependable, hard-working, and organized. The Ones are very different from the next personality type of the Enneagram structure, which is the Type Two - The Helper.

The next chapter will cover every aspect of The Helper personality type.

Chapter 4: Type Two - The Helper

The Type Two or The Helper, as the late Riso had stated in his book, *Personality Types: Using the Enneagram for Self-Discovery*, is the type to be there for anyone to help them because that is exactly what they are - helpers. They are there at any time for anyone in need. They are extremely selfless and put their needs last. They are all about love, and they are the types that would remember the birthdays and anniversaries of others whether they are family members, co-workers, acquaintances or friends.

They are extremely warm and caring and are very emotional. Their homes are always welcome to others and will be the first to cook up a hearty meal to anyone in need. And this trait would be seen in early childhood. Children don't normally develop empathy until they are in grade 3 or 4 because they are only aware of themselves and are only aware of their own needs before that. However, the Twos have shown empathy even at a very young age. Even as babies they would have shown empathy of some sort by snuggling up to any of their caregivers and giving them a kiss on the cheek to the best of their ability.

As toddlers, Twos would give plenty of hugs and would have shown love to animals and even to younger babies. As children, they would have begged their parents for a pet to cuddle and they would also be kind of their younger siblings. As the Twos became older and started going to school, they would also be the first to befriend anyone. Especially the underdog. And they may have been the underdog as well which would have increased their empathetic feelings for those who also had an obvious rough time.

Twos most definitely spend a lot of their energy caring for the needs of others, and the trap that they can easily fall into is becoming burned out by putting their needs last. And whenever that happens to anyone, they learn the hard way that they cannot pour out of an empty cup. However, you would think that the Twos based on their traits would be the ultimate saints. You would think that they are giving and caring without expecting anything back from anyone because from what you had just read, that appears to be their nature.

The Twos may be selfless, caring, empathetic, and are there to put the needs of others first before them. However, they don't do it without any ulterior motives. They expect to be appreciated and expect others to give back as well by appreciating them. They don't expect to be given material gifts, but if they feel at all that they are being taken for granted, they will not let that go. They expect you to thank them in a genuine way. They will expect that you have them over for dinner or dessert as well to thank them for their kindness and selflessness. They want to be needed, and they want to help, but it comes with a cost.

In fact, if they feel that they are not being appreciated and are not given back what they had given out, they can become abusive, irrational, and quite hysterical. As long as they feel that they have been compensated for their efforts in the ways that satisfied them, they will continue to be there for others to help in any way possible.

They would not expect to be given back what they had given out to those who they know are not capable of doing so or are quite incapacitated such as caring for animals, babies and young children, the elderly, the ill, and the disabled whether it would be physical or mental. That is because the Twos know that those in this group cannot give back and they genuinely help those in this group because again, they love to be needed and those that fall in this category are naturally dependent.

They would also give a free pass to those who are in an

authoritative position such as a parent or even more so their bosses. They know that they have to be at their best with their bosses. However, if they are happy with what they are earning at work, then they will be happy to give more to their bosses. If their bosses are asking them to do tasks that the Twos do not feel compensated for on a constant basis, then they will start to look for another job behind their backs.

However, when it comes to fully functional adults as well as older children and teenagers, they will expect them to show their appreciation towards them for their efforts. Otherwise, they will not be kind and will become quite nasty towards them. They expect to receive the same love that they had given to others, and the reason behind this ulterior motive that the Twos have is because if they are not given back the love they had given and are not appreciated- then it blemished their self-image. This is a huge threat to them. This is why they become abusive, irritational and inconsolable.

Other than that, because of the ultimate giving nature, they will only work in jobs that are fitting for their personality type. In the next section, the description of their ideal jobs and how they behave in the workplace will be covered.

Twos In The Workplace

The late Riso had stated in his book, Personality Types: Using the Enneagram for Self-Discovery that the Twos are all about helping others and wanting to be needed by others, even with their ulterior motive. The way the Twos would behave in the workplace would be no different from any other setting.

A typical day at work for the Type Two would be leaving home to head to work. And if he or she is driving and sees that a driver on the other lane wants to pass, of course, the Two would slow down and allow the driver to pass because again, anyone else's needs are put ahead of their own. And if the driver thanks the Two by using the hand gesture that indicates a thank you, then the Two will be happy to have received that kind gesture from the driver on the road.

If the driver, however, does not thank the Two, then the Two will become aggressive by honking at the driver that he or she allowed to pass, or even worse, giving the driver the finger and screaming profanities even though the other driver wouldn't hear it. Maybe the Two would even go as far as purposely tailgating the driver. Either way, the Two would expect to be thanked even on the way to work or anywhere else they are going.

And, once the Two type goes to the office, he or she will begin to start working as expected. However, it will be a matter of time that a co-worker is in need of some help for some reason. Perhaps they had run out of paper and are unsure of where to look for extra paper or other supplies. The Two will immediately stop what he or she is doing and will go out of his or her way to help the co-worker find the paper or the supplies that are needed. More often than not, the co-worker will thank the Two type, and that will be enough for the Two to get back to work because of being satisfied for being thanked for his or her efforts in regard to helping the co-worker find the supplies needed.

If the co-worker doesn't thank the Two type properly, then he or she will become angry and will be simmering. Because of the fact that he or she knows to behave at work in order to keep the job, the Type Two will not scream and yell at the co-worker for the lack of appreciation. Instead, he or she will display passive-aggressive behaviors towards the ungrateful co-worker such as being extremely sarcastic. And the co-worker would not understand why the Type Two was being incredibly nasty and did not realize that the explanation for the nasty treatment was due to not showing appreciation for The Helper's efforts.

And, what would end up happening is that The Helper

would simmer about not being shown appreciation and allow it to fester all day at work, and on the way home. This is where the Twos would get into trouble when it comes to their work environment. If they do not feel appreciated by their co-workers for something, they went out of their way to do, then they become angry and allow their intense irate feelings fester. That means the quality of their work would suffer due to being too distracted from being angry about the fact that they were taken for granted, which they believe.

That means in order for the Twos to perform well at the job, they have to feel that any of their co-workers that they had gone out of their way to help appreciated them for their efforts. Otherwise, their sour feelings towards their ungrateful co-workers would hurt their performance.

Aside from that, the type of careers that the Twos are best suited for since they are extremely people-oriented are:

- Providing therapy
- Teaching
- Doctor
- Nurse

- Sales

- Bartending

- Waiting

- Publishing

- Advice Columnist

- Matchmaking

- Writing

And, the Twos are happy to provide as much as they can to others in the work they do because they are being paid. That is the compensation they need, and they don't need their patie4nts or clients to thank them for their hard work if they are getting paid.

The types of jobs the Twos must avoid are:

- Editor

- Tax agent

- Agent

- Officer

- Admissions for college

Now you know how the Twos are in a working environment. In the final section of this chapter, the way their relationships end up will be covered more in-depth than how it has previously.

Twos And Their Relationships

Twos will do anything to make sure that the needs of their lovers, their friends, and as stated above, their co-workers are met. However, there is an ulterior motive. That is because they have to feel appreciated for their selfless duties and for the sacrifices they have made for them. If not, then they became abusive, irrational, and end up in hysterics.

The lack of compensation threatens their core and their self-image reflects literally the type that they are - The Helper. They want to help but expect to be thanked. When their children are little, they will not expect anything back from them because of the fact that they are not capable of giving back. However, as their children age and mature, that changes.

The Twos will eventually expect to be appreciated by their own children once they are old enough to understand how to give back. In fact, many teenage and adult children of the Twos end up cutting them out because of how their parents really don't give of themselves of the goodness of their hearts. The only times that the Twos will not place any expectations on children if they have special needs.

Yet that also depends on the severity of the disability as well. If the child is mildly disabled whether it is mental or physical, the same demands will be placed on that child as they would be on their typical siblings. If the disability is severe or profound, then they will not be expected to give back because they cannot.

It would also not be surprising to learn that many Twos end up in failed marriages because of their expectations and demands for being appreciated. Many friends that they had would have also given up on them for the fact that they are too demanding and may even find the Twos quite draining. The Twos suffer at work as well as in relationships of all kinds.

The next personality type of the Enneagram is the Type 3 - The Performer who will be covered in the following chapter.

Chapter 5: Type 3 - The Performer

The third personality type that is talked about in many sources which include the late Riso's book, *Personality Types: Using the Enneagram for Self-Discovery*, is the Type Three personality or The Performer. If you think that the performer has a knack for performing music or anything that is related, that could be fitting - as long as they are the cream of the crop.

The Threes or the Performers are also known as the Achievers. And if you now have a better idea of what personality type they are, and you have guessed that they are constantly improving their performance no matter what it may be in because as long as they are successful, then they are happy - you are right.

The Threes are constantly upping their game only to be successful. And it can be anything from being them being the best-looking person around with that perfectly toned body in their social circle or them becoming a millionaire or just the best at anything that is important to them that they do. The frequently compare their success to others, and they are highly competitive because they will not accept anything other than reaching the top.

This personality type may sound like it is parallel to the Ones, and to some degree it is. The difference is that the Ones are just obsessed with perfection in general. They aren't particularly looking to be the best-looking individual or the wealthiest around per se. The Ones just want to have everything in their lives perfect because they can't rest if there is any disorganization or disarray which causes perfection. They feel like the ultimate failures if they don't achieve perfection, and they are not gregarious.

The Threes, however, aren't looking for perfection per se other than then being the best in what they do, and they are actually quite gregarious and extroverted. For instance, the Ones would become upset if the house was not clean and organized because that means the house is not in tip top perfect shape. The Threes would not be concerned about that unless they were striving to become the best housekeepers. In other words, the Threes are only looking for perfection when it comes to their own achievements, not when it comes to anything else.

That means that the Threes are constantly bettering their performance in anything that is important to them so they can attain success. That is what is validating to their self-image. As long as they are successful in whatever it is that is important to them, then they feel secure. They also are quite likable which was already mentioned, they are charismatic, and are the types that are known to be the most popular at school.

This personality type is also seen from early childhood once they begin to gain awareness. The Threes really start to stand out when they start school, even as early as kindergarten. If they are given an art project to do, they would have done anything they could to make their artwork stand out better than the artwork created by their classmates. And if any of their classmates did a better job than they did, then that would have upset the Threes to the core - even in kindergarten.

As the Threes matured and evolved throughout school, then that would apply to them being the best at sports. In fact, if they were playing baseball during a physical education session, not only would they have insisted that their team won - but they would have insisted on being the reason that their baseball team won. The Threes had to be the ones to achieve that winning home run or else they would feel like the ultimate loser, and that means they would feel invalidated. Even if their baseball team at school had won.

The same goes for them having the need to be the most popular kid at school, and the best-looking, and the one to be able to get the boy or girl of their dreams to date. Not all Threes in school cared about getting the best grades if that was not at all important to them, and that is also what makes this personality type different from the Ones. That would only apply to the Threes that cared about being the best of their class academically, and in that case, they would strive to become the valedictorian. For the Threes that care about being the best performers academically, and did not make it to the valedictorian status, they would feel like the ultimate failure and loser.

Threes appear to be confident because they are quite extroverted and usually dress quite well, even if they are not concerned about being the prettiest or the most handsome person around. However, they are actually extremely insecure and are afraid to become intimate because that means they would end up exposing their vulnerabilities if they were. No matter how much success the Threes have achieved, it will not be good enough because every failure they encountered sticks to them. That means if they were intimate, then their past failures could be seen which is the last thing that they want to see happen.

If the Threes feel threatened in any way by any type of competition, they become ruthless, narcissistic, and will not care who gets hurt as long as they attain their goals- and beat their competition. Their sense of morals would disappear and would be happy to throw anyone under the bus for whatever reason.

Here is a scenario. A Three is a master internet marketer and partnered up with someone who is well-known in the internet marketing community to create an elite course on SEO. The Three had intended to make this course the cream of the crop- better than the ones out there! And, the intention was to have the course launched by a certain date if that meant that a competitor was going to be releasing a similar course around the same time. That meant the course had to be released well before the competitor was going to release their course in SEO.

A date was chosen, and the partner of the Three had to be present during the time of the release. However, on the day of the release, the partner had gotten sick, or one of the family members had to be taken to the hospital. This meant the partner was not going to be able to be present during the release date. This meant having to delay the release of the course. The Three would not stand for that because that would mean the competitor would end up releasing their SEO course before the Three did.

That means the Three would release the course anyway

behind the partner's back and would end up taking all of the credit instead of even acknowledging the partner's expertise in SEO. This had to happen so the course would be released long before the competitor had released theirs. The Three would not care whether or not the partner had a personal emergency to tend to which was the reason that the course had to be delayed. The Three had to win because that was the only way that his or her self-image could be protected. If the competitor's course had come out before the Three's did, and if others found it to be quite valuable, then they would have no need to purchase Three's course - and the worst could happen as well!

The competitor could potentially end up as the master in SEO because his or her course was released first. That would not be acceptable to the Three.

You have an idea of how the Three would behave in the workplace which will be covered more in detail in the next section of this chapter.

Threes In The Workplace

It is quite easy to imagine how competitive the Three type would be among co-workers. They have to be the employee of the month each and every month and will do anything possible to make that happen. That even means them telling their bosses the things that their co-workers did to get them into trouble in order to make sure that they are the employees of the month. That also would mean that if they remained as their boss' favorite employee, then they would be the first ones chosen to receive a promotion.

After all, that is what the Threes want. They want to keep climbing up the corporate ladder. They want to keep striving for betterment only so they truly are considered as the best of the best. Failure is not an option, because if a peer or a co-worker outperforms the Three, then that will cause the Performer to feel like the ultimate loser. That is something that cannot be handled at all costs.

That means that working with a Three type co-worker would be a nightmare. The Three would be the type to bully him or her if she or he was a threat to the Three's success in any way at all. The Threes would also be the best fitting for certain job types and would not a poor fit for other jobs.

The list of careers that best fit the type Three are:

- Producer
- News or any type of journalist

- Disk jockey
- Attorney
- Literary agent
- Sports agent
- Entertainer
- Beauty-related
- Author
- Internet marketer (because it is competitive)

The worst types of jobs would be for the Threes are:

- Freelance writing since there is no need to strive to be the top of the competition
- Running an Etsy store or being self-employed that does not encourage career advancement

In fact, the Threes would do poorly when it comes to any type of free-form career advancement because they have nothing to show off. If they do better with their own businesses and no one would know the difference, then that is not validating enough to them to see themselves as successful.

This also means Threes would struggle when it comes to their personal relationships which include family which will be covered in the next chapter.

Threes And Relationships

If you have guessed that the Three- type personality would struggle to maintain relationships, then you are right because of the fact that they are afraid to be intimate. That means they make themselves vulnerable to anyone. They don't ever want to show their failures or insecurities in general to anyone. Especially if the Three is extremely concerned about their own body image and they don't want to expose their less-than-perfect parts of their bodies to anyone.

However, for the Threes that aren't concerned about their body image may have a little bit of an easier time being intimate and forming relationships. It all depends on the area that the Threes care about advancing. Unfortunately, many of them end up in failed marriages or relationships. That is because if the Three received a promotion from work which meant an opportunity for them to move out of town to advance their career- and their significant other had held them back, then the Three would rather throw the relationship away than pass up that golden opportunity to help them validate themselves.

Here is a scenario. The Three was married to someone who had a sick parent to tend to which meant that the spouse was constantly taking the parent to doctor's appointments. The Three also had received an opportunity through work to advance the career which meant the family had to relocate. However, the spouse could not consider leaving the city at the time because of having to care for the sick parent. The spouse might have another concern about that as well, which is the worry about not finding a job so quickly if the relocation happened. The Three would not stand for that and would file for divorce and take off anyway.

This means that advancing their career is so important to them that family comes second. The Three would also even consider leaving the kids behind with the spouse in this situation as well if the kids held them back.

Speaking of kids, the Three's kids would have a difficult time meeting his or her approval. That is because the Performer expects success not just from him or herself, but from the kids. It is not uncommon for children of the Three-type to cut themselves off from the Performer parent when they reach adulthood for this reason. Their kids would refer them to as being narcissistic and toxic parents. That would also mean that if the Three had a child with special needs, then that in itself would be the ultimate failure.

Producing a less-than-perfect child would be scarring to the Three's self-image and would not even consider working with the child. The Three would likely want to give the child up for adoption or to surrender the child to the state and would want to forget about the fact that the child was even born. This is just another example of how the Three could be ruthless if their self-image was at the risk of being tarnished.

When it comes to friendships, the Threes would have a difficult time maintaining friendships as well if they had held their opportunities for success back in any way. This is quite apparent that attaining and achieving success is more important than personal relationships.

The next personality type in the Enneagram model that will be covered in the next chapter is the Type 4 - The Romantic.

Chapter 6: Type 4- The Romantic

The Type Four personality or The Romantic as it is stated in the late Riso's book, *Personality Types: Using the Enneagram for Self-Discovery*, is also referred to as The Individualist. Fours are known to be extremely creative, idealistic, very empathetic, and make their unique selves known. They are also nonconformist.

In fact, they create their own identities based on their own perceptions of being different from the rest. They see their differences from others as both a good thing and a bad thing. They see it as a positive thing because they do not like to be considered as clones or as sheep. However, the negative thing about this aspect is that Fours often feel that they are unable to feel the same types of pleasures and happiness that others feel from common things.

Examples of those are enjoying the simple things such as a sunny day, a freshly brewed cup of coffee, or a glass of wine. It is not that Fours don't enjoy those things, but they get a lot more enjoyment from anything that is more complex. It frustrates them that they cannot experience the same kind of pleasure that others experience from the simple things in life.

That being said, Fours realize they are complex beings, and they consider that to be both a blessing and a curse. They suffer from both a superiority and an inferiority complex. They think that they are both "better" than others, but at the same time, they envy others for a variety of reasons.

They think they are superior over others because of the fact that they are not a clone like most people are. However, they long for the simpler lives that people live. In fact, their feelings towards others go from feeling superior over them feeling shameful and defective compared to them. As it is said, Fours are extremely complex.

They often feel misunderstood which adds to their frustration and have a strong desire to be understood, which they feel they never are, and quite often they feel unappreciated. They are extremely moody, temperamental, can be quite melodramatic and melancholic. They have a tendency to withdraw from others and stay in their own world. Their own world is the only place that makes sense to them. Their own place in their heads is the only place where they can seek sanctuary because the real world is cold and crude which they cannot be a part of because it is extremely overwhelming, and their hearts cannot take it.

Fours also badly miss people and situations that failed to work out for them and fantasize about those people or situations coming back. They fantasize about the future as well. They do this to escape in general. This aspect is what also makes the Four type personality quite empathetic.

Fours are extremely sensitive and have a soft spot for the underdog, for the weak, and for animals. They are prone to mental illness such as depression and addiction because they are constantly looking for external ways to bring them relief from their chronic inner woes. They can easily drink, eat, and do drugs and become addicted to all of it. Some, unfortunately, engage in self-harm such as cutting and can easily develop eating disorders.

The Romantic types are the ones that will easily express their feelings through forms of art such as painting, drawing, writing, music, and many of them are into body art. Those who are inked and have plenty of piercings are likely Fours because that is how they express their individualistic selves.

The Fours are also likely to be interested in unusual genres of music, television, books, and movies. They will only like a common genre of any of it if a particular song, show, movie, or book relates to them in any way. For instance, the average Four would scoff at chick flick movies or light-hearted comedies but would love to watch a farce, offbeat comedy movie such as the 1995 flick, *Four Rooms* that was directed by Quentin Tarantino.

They would also be likely to detest any type of pop music that is in the top 40 because it represents what everyone else likes. They would be drawn more towards genres such as thrash metal, punk, alternative, ambient, and house music. Any genre that represents uniqueness, just like who they are.

This personality type would show their individualistic side ever since early childhood as they would be the type to play with a spoon or an object as opposed to a common toy that other kids would like. They are the ones who likely were bullied and picked on during their school years because of being so different. They would respond by withdrawing more and going into their own safe world. They would have had the most difficult time during their middle school years until the end of high school.

Fours would have both been likely to be disgusted by the popular crowd because of them being clones, yet at the same time would have been envious for them for having such easy lives - as they had perceived.

Depending on how the Fours would have responded to their bullies, they would have either drowned more into their sorrows and could have ended up ending up at a very bad place - or they would have rebelled and told them off in their own way by continuing to be themselves and by going into their faces.

Based on the idealistic type and individualistic type of The Romantic, you would assume that the Fours would not end up working at any conventional job. In the next section of this chapter, the Fours and the workplace will be covered more in depth.

Fours In The Workplace

If you had guessed that the Fours would not mesh well in conventional workplace settings, that guess is right. Fours would be quite miserable in a typical 9 to 5 work environment. As it was previously mentioned, Fours are idealistic and do not always think in practical terms that they would need to work in a company that is stable in order to earn the money they need to survive.

Many Fours become artists as they rely on art in order to express themselves as many are creative writers, musicians, and artists of other types. The problem with that is that money may not be made at all by relying on those unstable career types.

Even though that is the case, most Fours do realize they need to have a steady job of some sort as they are in reality enough to know they have to earn some kind of reliable income to get by. They need money to eat, to pay rent or a mortgage if they actually were fortunate enough to buy a home or a condo, and they need to pay for their utility expenses. However, they still hope to become successful musicians, artists, or writers one day. And they would only work in the following types of more or less reliable jobs in order to survive:

- Hairstyling
- Manicurist
- Pedicurist
- Salon worker
- Tattoo artist
- Yoga teacher
- Therapist, because they can relate to those who are struggling with their mental health, and can find a way to help them

- Masseuse

- Reflexologist

- Acupuncturist

- Creative writing instructor

- A clerk at a New Age store

- Graphic designer

- Freelance writer

- Internet marketer

- Marketing and advertising without selling personally

- Content creation for social media managers

- Entrepreneur because they would be excellent marketers and could easily brand themselves in a unique way

They readily take on roles of those jobs while they work on the side writing a book, creating music, or doing artwork on the side. They still fantasize that they would be best-sellers one day, or highly popular musicians or successful artists. However, most Fours do realize that they need to have a stable job as the ones that are the most fitting in order to live.

The worst possible jobs that the Fours could end up falling into are:

- Any kind of 9 to 5 job at any office
- Anything administrative
- Police officer
- Stockbroker
- Accounting
- Law
- Medicine
- Any job that has to be based on the rules or standards of someone else

The only exception to this is if they were hired by a company as a marketer or advertiser that has nothing to do with sales. They would come up with the creative marketing ideas so that a sales representative could use.

Based on all that has been said, Fours would not mix well with other co-workers as they only want to work alone unless they are serving clients in job roles that are the most suitable to them which was mentioned above.

You may also wonder if the Fours are complete loners that would never want to get married, let alone to be in a relationship; however, that is not always the case. The last section of this chapter will cover Fours and their relationship types.

Fours And Relationships

Based on what you would have learned about The Romantic type is that they would never want to be in a relationship at all. Because of their extreme individualistic nature, they would be the type to live a solo life and have the freedom to do what they want while they are living in a studio apartment. However, that is not always the case.

Many Fours actually do want to be in relationships, and that only has to do with the fact that they would become lonely if they did not have a mate. It is true that they would not want to be in a relationship because of society's expectations. They want to be with partners for the sake of not being alone for the rest of their lives. And, they would be quite picky with who they would be in a relationship with.

They would not want to hook up with someone who was

concerned with meeting society's standards. In other words, they would not want to be in a relationship with anyone who would not have a mind of their own. Fours are naturally not attracted to clones. They would only hook up with those who embraced their own unique ways and rebelled towards society's expectations. That is the most attractive trait that the Fours are looking for which goes for them looking for their life partners as well as the friends they want to make.

Fours may be individualistic, but they still need human interaction. Many are hermits and only socialize on their own terms. And many of them do get married because that is what they want for their own reasons, not for pleasing anyone else. Many Fours also go and have kids of their own, and they are the ones that teach their kids to embrace their uniqueness. They will teach their kids to follow their hearts and not to allow themselves to be pressured by anyone else in life.

And, as much as Fours detest rules in general, they will tell their kids to respect elders and to be respectful towards others because it is the right thing to do. Morals are morals and Fours want their kids to have morals and to be kind. Fours would also likely be able to nurture a child with special needs properly because they naturally are empathetic towards the underdog in general. They would teach a child with exceptional needs on how to embrace themselves in their best ability.

Fours are idealistic, nonconforming, highly creative, extremely emotional, and only want to engage with others that are also quite individualistic. They are also once again attracted to the underdog and will have a lot of sympathy and empathy towards those who have lived colorful and harsh lives. They detest society and its standards and will not have anything to do with those who are seen as popular or who have had a life that did not present them a lot of challenges. The next personality type that will be covered in the following chapter is The Type 5 personality, which is The Investigator.

Chapter 7: Type 5 - The Investigator

Those who are in the Type Five group or the ones who are referred to as The Investigator type have some similarities to the Fours but are also quite different. As the late Riso had stated in his book, *Personality Types: Using the Enneagram for Self-Discovery,* Fives are those who observe, gain knowledge and wisdom through observing and experiences. However, they keep themselves. They keep away from human interaction because they do not want to be part of the drama at any cost.

Fives are known to be extremely analytical, private, unobtrusive, self-sufficient, and are very thoughtful. They spend their lives gaining knowledge as well as wisdom. Those who are in the Investigator group are quite independent, objective, are the types to be calm when it comes to any kind of crises, and they are highly intelligent because they are always very busy taking in information.

However, as observant and as intelligent as they are, the Fives are quite detached and finds ways to protect themselves from those that can pose some kind of risk to them or from those who may end up asking too much. They also come off as quite eccentric, indifferent, they never want to intrude or be in anyone's way at all which even means they will suffer in silence and are withdrawn and shy.

That means even if they genuinely needed someone's help, they would not want to ask for it due to the fear that they would be obtrusive. This even includes medical emergencies unless it is a matter of life and death, then they would know they would not have a choice but to go to the ER or to their doctor. Otherwise, they would rather find a way to heal themselves even though they may not be in the medical field themselves. But since they are the types to have the constant hunger to learn, they would spend time researching how to heal an illness or a condition that does not necessarily need the help of a doctor.

The one thing that the Fives want more than anything is to understand the reasons behind everything, how things work and are the types to want to be able to give the right answer to any question that is asked. They are extremely terrified deep down from being helpless and incompetent. In fact, they are incredibly sensitive. And in order to mask this sensitive side, they make it known that they are indifferent and will not hesitate to show off their intellect. They also know their social skills are weak and they show off their smarts to overcompensate for that truth. That means the Fives can easily become intellectually arrogant which will only repel others, which is what they want anyway since they have no time or patience for human interaction.

The Investigator personality would show up in early childhood. The youngster would show immediate interest in learning even as older infants. Even though babies are naturally curious as it is because they are learning about the world around them, the Fives would show an intense interest in learning during toddlerhood by constantly looking at age-appropriate books, as well as having the need to solve age-appropriate puzzles and stacking toys.

They also would not have any desire to play with other kids or parallel play. This may alarm parents because these are the traits that professionals look for that can be indicative of an autism spectrum disorder such as Asperger's Syndrome. However, not all Fives are on the spectrum, as many neurotypical individuals possess the Investigator personality.

Once the Fives enter kindergarten and are in early grade school, their thirst and hunger for learning become more intense. They will want to borrow books from the library that will offer them something intellectual to read and to stay so they can gain knowledge. They have no time for fiction or fantasy books because they are not learning anything from reading those books and it does not stimulate their intellect. Any kind of fiction that the Fives accept is Sci-Fi. That keeps their brains stimulated.

The Fives have always been the type during childhood to read a book, or even get a head start on doing homework while sitting in a corner by themselves during recess. While the other kids are outside playing with each other, the Fives keep to themselves. The Investigator would be known as that straight-A student and as the teacher's pet. In later elementary school, and during junior high, they would become targets of bullying because of this, and the other kids would call them nerds or geeks.

When the Fives enter high school, this trait becomes even more intense as they keep maturing. At that point, they could be bullied even more viciously because of the fact that not only are they considered as the nerds, but their peers would pick up on the eccentricities that the Fives possess.

That also means that because the Fives come off as eccentric, unfeeling, and are only concerned with tools such as books, computers, or anything else to feed their brains - they actually have a lot more feelings underneath that outer shell that is projected. They have some similar traits to the Fours, however, unlike the Fours, Fives are not comfortable with expressing themselves in any way at all whereas the Fours do with body art, or through painting, writing, or through music. Fives would prefer to disappear from the world if they had a choice in order to not make themselves known at all.

Fives have an easier time socially at university because of the fact that they will go into a field such as medicine, science, engineering and anything else that requires more devotion to the study rather than with human interaction. They will be placed in classes with peers that are studying the same field, which means it is likely that many of their classmates are Fives as well and would keep to themselves as a result.

If you are wondering how Fives interact at work, and what the best career choices are, that will be covered in the next section of this chapter.

Fives In The Workplace

It would not come to anyone as a surprise that the typical Five would work in any field that is the most fitting for their type alone and behind the scenes. They really don't want to be seen and intrude in any way at all. That means

Fives will not be at all suitable for any type of office environment and would not work a typical 9 to 5 job at all. In fact, the best types of career-roles for the Fives are:

- Engineering
- Anything to do with technology
- Game and app design
- Researcher
- Analyst
- Scientist
- Mathematician
- Astronomer
- Lab technician
- Professor (only when it comes to teaching university students fields in any of the above listed)

Fives have the capacity and interest to go into medicine. However, they would not make good doctors because that means they have to interact and treat patients. However, they could possibly become pharmacists which means they will still have to interact with patients picking up prescriptions. Though the level of interaction they would have with people is reduced.

The worst career-choices for Fives are:

- Any field that requires them to interact with people
- Publicist
- Hospitality
- Retail
- Waiting
- Bartending
- Teaching high school and elementary school
- Childcare

Many Fives like animals but they would also not become veterinarians because of having to deal with pet owners. However, if their dealings with people were limited, some may agree to become veterinary technicians if they happen to have a strong interest in animals.

At the same time, Fives would not care about the niche they would work in if they had an engineering job that meant they would be behind the scenes. For instance, many Fives work as engineers at radio stations, a setting where there is a lot of human interaction whether it would be by the phone or those in the area visiting the radio announcers. Fives don't care about that as long as they are away from people while working with the machinery.

Here is another example of what form of work setting is ideal for the majority of Fives. Fives that are scientists, engineers, or technicians would grab at the chance to winter over at a remote setting such as Concordia Station in Antarctica which is literally out in the middle of nowhere. The weather is the most severe in this area as well, especially during the long and very dark winter. They would have to work with those in the same setting as them in that particular building. However, they usually don't have a problem with that since those who they are working with are likely other Fives and will only socialize when it suits them.

That means you would also wonder based on what was said about the Fives that they would be complete hermits since they avoid social contact at all costs. However, this is not always the case. More about Fives and relationships will be covered in the last section of this chapter.

Fives And Relationships

Based on what has been covered on the Fives, people may think of them as hermits that spend their entire lives studying, reading intellectually stimulating books for the rest of their lives. However, the fact of the matter is that one of the basic needs for everyone regardless of their personality type is engaging in social interaction. Even the Fives themselves are aware of this. The complete lack of social interaction can induce mental illnesses and other illnesses. It is a basic need, just as how clothing, food, water, and shelter are.

Fives will also not close themselves off if they happen to come across those who are just like them. If they come across another Investigator type, then they will let go of the insecurities of their poor social skills and actually be confident enough to be themselves. That is because if they come across anyone who is just like themselves, then they can be free. There is nothing preventing them from being closed-off. Think back to that example of the scientists and technicians hanging out with one another at the remote Antarctic Concordia Station.

When Fives connect with those who are just like themselves, there is no worry about the lack of understanding and any threat that is perceived due to being around other people disappears. When you have a group of Fives together in one room, then they will hang together, and watch Sci-Fi movies, and laugh and joke around with one another. They don't care that their sense of humor would be considered off-beat because the others around them would completely appreciate it. And, yes, that means, Fives actually do have a sense of humor, but it never comes out unless they are in a setting with other Fives.

The thing about friendships and Fives is that once the Investigator makes a friend, then that friend is one for life. Many Fives have also gotten married and have had children. They would only connect with those who were just like them, just as the Fours would.

However, once Fives do get married and have children, the problems they could run into are when their kids begin to go to school. This means their kids parents, the Investigators, will need to be interacting with the teachers. Especially when problems arise, and that is a guarantee at some point.

Fives as parents may discourage their kids from being part of any kind of group because that is how they are. This could be a disservice to their kids, especially if their kids are more extraverted. However, Fives will stress the importance of making a good lifelong friend as long as the right type of friend is connected.

You have learned a lot about the Fives in this chapter. In the next chapter, the next personality type in the Enneagram model will be covered. That is Type 6 - The Loyalist.

Chapter 8: Type 6 - The Loyalist

Those in the Type Six group are also referred to as The Loyalists as it is stated in the late Riso's book, *Personality Types: Using the Enneagram for Self-Discovery*. Those who have this personality type indicated on the Enneagram model are extremely insecure, paranoid, anxious, nervous, and are very distrusting. They are always worried about what could possibly go wrong and have a hard time believing that anything actually can turn out just fine.

Sixes do not at all trust easily and have a strong sense of suspicion with no matter who is approaching them, and don't trust that any situation will have a good outcome. However, because of this constant state of worrying, Sixes are quite good at troubleshooting in general. But the anxiety and fear that they are living through as a result of their constant worrying, distrust, and suspicion engulfs them and prevents them from relaxing and enjoying anything and anyone.

The core reason that the Sixes are highly suspicious, anxious, and distrusting is that they are longing to look for something or someone they can trust. And those who have successfully proven themselves trustworthy to the Loyalist would have done something extraordinary since Sixes are so naturally distrusting.

Those who have earned the trust of any of the Sixes really would have had to move mountains to gain their trust. The unfortunate thing is that if the individual who had successfully gained the Loyalist's trust had done something to break it, then the Six would still continue to trust that individual. That even means that if the individual had left the Six's life as a result, the Six would still hang onto false hope that there is still something trustworthy about that individual - or even a situation if the situation had let the Six down after he or she had invested that energy to trust it. That is because it would shatter the Six if he or she came to terms with the fact that something or someone who he or she had struggled to trust actually did ruin it. Then that would be a sign that absolutely nothing or no one is trustworthy at all.

And because the Six is constantly looking for something or to someone to really believe in, they tend to become obsessed with something or someone who they think has the potential to give them what they need, which is their reason to trust them. This can easily get the Six into trouble as well. They could end up trusting the wrong person or thing, and they are more likely not going to be able to trust anyone who has their best interest at heart, or who are doing their job to help them.

For instance, the Loyalist would be difficult patients for doctors. That is because the Six would not at all trust what doctors are prescribing to them. Sixes would immediately think that they are being poisoned or that the doctor is giving them something that would purposely not help them which may be due to their personal gain.

Examples of the types that would fit into this group are those who believe in conspiracy theories such as the Earth being flat. This group has constantly expressed their distrust towards organizations such as NASA and believe that they are only gaining something by stating that the Earth is not flat. They have been accused by those that believe in this theory as manufacturing pictures of the Earth from space through CGI technology - which did not exist on this level in the 1960s when those images were first starting to come out.

Additionally, they will always believe that the Earth is flat even though there is no proof. This is a belief they will keep hanging onto because the nature of this personality type is to hold onto any idea that they believe must be true even though evidence everywhere has pointed out that there is no truth to this theory. The Sixes would dismiss those who have proof that their belief is false and accused them of saying those things for their own personal gain - even though that is the furthest from the truth. Remember, this group is called The Loyalist group for a reason. They don't trust easily and are yearning to believe in something and are yearning to trust something which means they will easily fall for the wrong thing or person!

The Loyalist group as children would have had severe separation anxiety since infancy, which is common for all babies regardless of how they end up turning out personality wise. However, the separation anxiety from their caregivers would last for a much longer time than it would for a child that is of another personality type. This type of separation anxiety would have caused them problems when they had entered school as well.

Eventually, they would have grown out of the infantile separation anxiety but would have still been quite anxious when it came to those who they believed were trustworthy leaving their side. And they would have a hard time making friends, for this reason, however, if a peer had proven to be trustworthy to them, then their trust would have been earned, or won.

If the Six did successfully make a friend during any stage of life whether it was during childhood or adulthood, then he or she would become anxious if their friend did not text them or call them at a certain time. And the Six would as a result always be the type to hover around their trusted friend because of the fact that they have to make sure that they really are trustworthy. Again, after all, the Six really did put a lot of their suspicions aside to be open to trusting that individual so that means the individual cannot let them down at all. And as it was mentioned before, the Six would still continue trusting the individual if he or she had let the Loyalist down due to hope and not wanting to face that that individual did let the Six down.

Sixes do have a hard time getting around in life because of their strong distrusting and anxious nature. This means their work and personal lives would be negatively affected as well. In the next section of this chapter, how Sixes are affected in the workplace will be covered in addition to the list of jobs that are ideal for this personality type.

Sixes In The Workplace

Sixes would have a difficult time at work as they would in all aspects of their lives. They would be the type to stay in a less than desirable job because they would fear to look for something better since there is always a catch of some sort. And for the Six to get the job that he or she is presently at, the employer would have had to gain their trust somehow. And even if the company that the Six is working for was decent at first, it does not mean it would stay that way. And even though the co-workers of the Six would have been looking for other jobs because of finding better opportunities, the Six would stay regardless.

The Six may know deep down that there may be something better out there. However, the suspicion of any other employer not being honest or the worry of coming into a problem at any new job would be greater than his or her willingness to look for a better opportunity. And the Six would have a very difficult time if he or she was laid off or fired because once again, false hope would be clenched onto by the Six. That would mean that the Six would keep hoping that the old employer would take him or her back, and even though that seldom happens, the Six would be unemployed for a long time.

The only thing that would motivate the Six looking for another job again is when the threat of eviction is very real because the Six would see that there is little money in the bank since it is not coming from anywhere else. This means the Six would think of looking for another job as biting the bullet and preparing him or herself from being let down by the future employer unless the employer actually proves themselves to be trustworthy. In that case, the Six will be comfortable at the job and will stay there as long as possible no matter how the working environment turns out.

If you had guessed that the Six would be a perfect fit for the predictable 9 to 5 office type of job, you are correct. That is the working environment that the Six feels the safest and the least threatened. Other job roles that the Sixes would be good for are:

- Writing

- Teaching preschool or elementary school children since they are not a threat

- Any type of job that involves animals since they are also not a threat

- Any type of job that involves activism since something positive can be created out of anything that causes frequent worrying

The worst type of jobs for the Sixes are:

- Financial planning

- Investing

- Law

- Any involvement with the food or hospitality and tourism industry

- Any type of job that involves risk-taking of any kind

And, the Sixes would have a hard time with personal relationships as this would have been quite easy to figure out. More of that will be covered in the next and final section of this chapter.

Sixes In Relationships

Based on the personality type of the Six, one would wonder if they would ever be in a position to get married or to end up in a serious relationship - or to even have friends at all. However, the answer to that question is, yes, for some Sixes they would end up having some friends and would end up getting married. Again, if the individual who has proven themselves to be trustworthy to the Six, then the Loyalist would be receptive.

However, the divorce rate for Sixes is low. That is because once they have earned trust, then it is very hard for the trust to go away even if some actions that their partners do causes them to be anxious such as not texting them in a timely manner. Unfortunately, there are many cases where the Sixes end up in abusive relationships because of the fear of leaving no matter how bad the situation is.

Anything extreme would have to happen in a relationship for the Six to have a desire to leave.

And in cases where the Six ends up leaving an especially bad relationship, he or she would likely remain single for life due to the fact that if one partner had really broken their trust, then any subsequent partners would do the same. Unfortunately, as well, Sixes as parents would not encourage their kids to take risks at all and may unintentionally put fear into them about not trusting others so easily. They would also tell their kids to never get their hopes up for anything, which can be good advice from a realistic standpoint since things in life rarely do turn out as planned.

Though, when a Loyalist parent tells his or her children to never get their hopes up, they are not referring to staying realistic about any situation. They are literally saying that they are guaranteed to be disappointed by everything in life and that there are very few things in life to trust. This becomes a complicated issue especially when the children are naturally risk-takers which the Six would have a very difficult time accepting.

It is safe to say that the Six only will stick to his or her comfort zone and will pass that way of thinking and believing onto their children - because it is safe, and like any other parent with good intentions, they want their kids to be safe as well. That sums up the Six personality type. In the next chapter, Type 7 or the Enthusiast will be covered.

Chapter 9: Type 7 - The Enthusiast

Have you come across individuals who are always excited about what is just around the corner? If so, are these people always looking forward to the next best thing to experience and are not acknowledging what is happening in the now? Or does this description apply to you? Then if you answered yes to any of that, then there is a personality type that matches this characteristic as well on the Enneagram model. This type is the Type Seven group or Enthusiasts.

As it said in the late Riso's book, Personality Types: Using the Enneagram for Self-Discovery, Sevens are always looking forward to the future and are really the ones who are making the most of their lives, sometimes to excess. Sevens are always very optimistic and do not accept any type of negativity at all in life, which includes failure. They have a need to live in constant excitement, and really do forget to stop and smell the roses.

This group is always living in the future, and this means that they will be constantly planning exciting trips or outings. That means after they take one trip, then they will be looking forward to taking the next, and so on. And once their excitement over those trips ends, then they will find something else to look forward to. Perhaps they will want to seek some type of adventure that they have never experienced, or they will go towards great lengths to meet a celebrity without taking in account that they will have to get through plenty of security to get to them.

Here is an example of what goes on with a Seven. He or she plans a trip to Africa to go on a safari which is an exciting opportunity that most people do not experience. However, once that trip is over, and even after gaining the experience of seeing a pride of lions closeup and personal, the Seven would forget that he or she had that experience and would then plan another trip to somewhere else such as India to see the Taj Mahal. And after that trip is over, then the same thing would happen again because this group is never appreciating what they had experienced and are always looking forward to the next best thing over and over again.

Even during the trip planning, the Seven would all of a sudden have an urge to go bungee jumping or skydiving or do something that the average individual would be apprehensive of doing. Part of their plans as well for the future is wanting to visit any celebrity by not even thinking about the fact that this type of thing is not at all easy to do - especially if you are just a random person that does not have any type of personal or business ties to the celebrity either. The Seven would be told this fact and would be warned that they would not be able to get through the tight security that is keeping the celebrity protected. The Seven's response would be to that "Who cares! They will let me in because this is part of my future plan and nothing will stop it from happening". Where is the logic to that? There is not any as that is unrealistic optimism which is what the Sevens are all about.

As you can imagine, they are highly energetic, extroverted, and are incredibly talented when it comes to multitasking as they can managing doing five jobs at once. In fact, they have an extreme spirit that is quite entrepreneurial as they can be highly successful business owners and are excellent networkers as well. They can be quite charming which is what attracts them to others.

However, it is a known fact that no one can stay so high for that long without crashing down, even the Seven and this is what gets them into trouble. The Sevens do anything they can possible to prevent themselves from experiencing a crash. And unfortunately, when they are faced with disappointments, they refuse to accept any of it. They are terrified of being in any kind of negative frame of mind and are the last group to be introspective. They will do anything they can to hang into any type of high as they will always magnify and even brag about their strengths and not acknowledge in any way at all that they have weaknesses.

Sevens do come off as narcissistic, and they can easily be prone to addictions for the sake of having that high feeling all the time. They can be addicted to shopping, gambling, food, alcohol, drugs or anything else that is clearly unhealthy. And the Sevens may be mistaken for the Three types. However, the main difference is that Threes have more of a one-track mind, unlike the Sevens.

The Sevens can also be mistaken for Fours when they are in their manic states which is often. However, the big difference with this is that Fours display that characteristic when they are embracing their pain which is behind them expressing themselves the way they do, and Sevens behave this way to escape from pain of any kind.

These traits would have been seen in early childhood. Kids that have the Seven personalities would appear to be spoiled because they would always beg their parents for a new toy and many times, they would successfully manipulate their parents into buying them the new toy they wanted. And that meant these children would quickly become bored with playing with the toys that their parents bought them and would always ask for new ones. For the ones whose parents refused would always have meltdowns over it. And they may have given up asking for new toys, but their adventure and pleasure-seeking personality would still show.

These are the kids that other parents fear that their kids would become involved with due to the fact that the young Seven would constantly get into trouble due to them always seeking new adventures and new thrills- which would, unfortunately, involve their peers since they are naturally extroverted. Sevens would be the types to experiment with drugs and alcohol at a young age, as well as getting into other forms of trouble. The average Enthusiast likely has been sent to the school's principal's office over and over again as well whereas the principals, the parents of the child, and the teachers would be stunned that the child would not learn his or her lesson after being in trouble so often.

That is because the Seven does not consider consequences and is just concerned about looking forward to the next adventure even if that means having to be in trouble and grounded over and over again. Seven children would be the type to be part of the popular crowd, and they would be the type of bully others for, unfortunately, the thrill, not considering how the victim would be affected at all. Sevens can be quite self-absorbed, and in order for them to be successful in the workplace, they would be the ones to seek jobs and go into fields that would make many people of different personality types uncomfortable.

Sevens In The Workplace

It is not hard to imagine that the Seven would take on career roles that would scare those with other personality types and the Seven would not at all do well in any type of routine 9 to 5 office type of job. They hate routine because routine lacks adventure and that is the Seven's worst nightmare.

They also know at the same time that they need to work in order to make money so they can live, but they will be very picky about the types of jobs they would have. Many of them would not want to take on a role that is looked down by others as well due to the fact that it could easily blemish their self-image. That being said, you will never see a Seven working in a factory, or stocking shelves in warehouses. There will be more about the types of jobs that clearly do not work for the Enthusiast soon. However, right now, the types of jobs that the Sevens are more suitable for are:

- Bartending
- Bar or nightclub owner
- Writing in the travel, beauty, or fashion niche
- Most job roles that involve travel or that are in the travel niche
- DJ
- Acting
- Photography that involves plenty of traveling
- Music publicist
- Small business owner
- Life coach
- Fitness instructor
- Working with celebrities even if that means taking a job that they would not normally take

The jobs that the Sevens would not be at all the best fit for other than the ones previously mentioned are:

- Medicine

- Law

- Customer service

- Accountant

- Clerical work of any sort unless a celebrity was involved

- Any job that involves routine

This is why it is rare to see Enthusiast co-workers unless you are also in bartending as the Seven would be, which would be the least exciting job that they would accept. And they would do so out of necessity as well. The Seven would not even attempt working in a setting that involves having to sit in cubicles next to other co-workers. This is also indicative of the fact that even though Sevens can be fun to be around, they many times do not last being in long-lasting relationships which will be covered in the next and last section of this chapter.

Sevens In Relationships

Sevens are naturally charismatic at first as they have an easy time making friends with those who are open to seeking adventure. The only time that Sevens repel others, in general, is when they start becoming condescending by bragging about their virtues, so they don't allow their faults to show. In other words, their narcissistic ways can be a huge repellant.

However, the problem with the Seven when it comes to personal relationships is that they seldom last due to the fact that the Seven would easily become bored with the partner and could not be tied down due to their nature. Unfortunately, this is the group that is the most prone to adultery due to being bored with their partner and seeking excitement from other places and sources. Some of them with more honest tendencies would not cheat and just file for divorce instead which is easier for the partner to handle due to the fact that no deception was involved.

The fact of the matter is that the only time when the Seven would stay in a committed relationship would be if he or she was in a serious relationship with someone else who was just like them, and constantly was looking for adventure and pleasure. In fact, some couples who are avid travelers who may have stayed together for a long time may likely both be Sevens as they would channel their adventure in a healthier manner.

The majority would not stick around with the partner for a long time, and that would even mean them taking off even if kids were involved. Sevens as parents may be either absent in order to indulge their need for consistent pleasure or would be the type to keep taking their kids out of school to go on trips and would not be concerned about committing truancy.

The likelihood that more often than not, Sevens do not get married because they fear being tied down and would go through great lengths to prevent that. Some are seen as commitment-phobic which they are, but it has nothing to do with them having bad past experiences with relationships. It all boils down to them taking off on a relationship that is becoming serious due to the fact that the Seven knows that if a marriage happened, then the fun would end, and rules would have to take its place.

That covers the Enthusiast personality type on the Enneagram model. The next personality type that will be covered in the next chapter is the Type 8 - The Challenger.

Chapter 10: Type 8 - The Challenger

The Type 8 group are those who are all about control, and any Eight is also called The Challenger. As it is stated in the late Riso's book, *Personality Types: Using the Enneagram for Self-Discovery*, Eights are literally all about control which has absolutely nothing to do with them being on any type of power trip for petty reasons.

Just like the Sevens, the Eights are extremely assertive, are always hungry for freedom, will not stand to be controlled in any way or form, and will bypass authority of any kind to attain it, and are incredibly energetic as well. However, the big difference between the Sevens and the Eights is that the Sevens are multi-focused as they are always looking for the next best thing. The Eights are power focused on one thing which they will go towards great lengths to attain what they are focused on, and they are also quite practical which the Sevens are not.

Eights not only refuse to be controlled by others but will not allow outside circumstances to have any kind of control over them. They absolutely do not accept the truth that there are situations in life that are out of one's hands. The Eights will do anything they can to manipulate anything just to have control over it which even includes doing something about any type of situation that normally would be out of one's hands.

However, this trait is not necessarily a negative thing if it is kept in control which would only be by the Eight agreeing to keep the trait in control for reasons of his or her own. For instance, if the Eight realized that he or she had extra weight to lose and had a desire to lose it, nothing would stop the Eight from attaining that goal because of the fact that they are in control of their health and their bodies.

Though, an Eight making the decision to lose weight would not be a common situation unless he or she had a reason of his or her own to make that change that had nothing to do with any type of the external influence. The Eight would never stand for that. That is because their appetites are hearty; they will indulge without feeling guilty or shameful in any way at all. Their instincts are also quite bold. And perhaps they need extra energy in order to keep going after their lofty goals which may be why their appetites are quite strong.

Based on what was written so far about the Eight personality type of the Enneagram model, you would think they would lack any type of vulnerability. However, just like the other personality types, Eights can be just as vulnerable and sentimental as the others. They also know this deep down, and they refuse to allow anyone to see it. They will never allow anyone to peg them as weak as they also refuse to lower their defenses in any situation. And, just like the Sixes, Eights do not trust easily either.

However, once the Eight do trust, then they can make a friend for life, and even become their fiercest protector if necessary. They can be loyal as well. Though, if the Eight is ever betrayed by anyone who he or she trusted, then the Challenger could become violent towards the offender. That is the difference between how the Sixes and the Eights handle being betrayed after being let down by the one who they had lowered their guards to trust.

The Sixes fantasize about a part of the offender being trustworthy again whereas the Eights will retaliate without any hesitation and can be emotionally or physically violent. They may be known as well for their gaslighting tactics.

This trait would have been easily detected in early childhood. The child may have been a quick developer as he or she would have had the instinct at an early age to become the master. It is not unusual for Type Eight toddlers to potty train quickly, but it would have been in their own terms. Not all Type Eight children would have wanted to master that skill so quickly just to be in control.

However, as the type Eight child matured and aged, they would have been the types to be high achievers and at the same time, popular but also would have not hesitated to bully those who they perceived as weak. They would have been the first ones to pick on peers who would have fit as Fours because of the fact that their eccentricities made them appear weak and would have caused them to be targeted.

Eights have a low tolerance for those who are perceived as weak as they have no compassion for them at all. Even though the Eights have been high achievers, they would have clashed with teachers due to power struggles. And many Eight boys in high school would have been the typical stereotypical jocks you would see. The girls would be the stereotypical cheerleaders who had the perfect body and would shame other girls who did not have a perfect figure as they did.

The Challengers would have been quite rebellious at home with their parents all due to once again, reasons that had to do with control. They would be the ones to never come home at their curfew hour because if they did, that would have meant they would have had to abide by their parents' rules which they would never have done. They would also find a way out of a situation that involved punishment by their parents as well. And Eights would have left home early so they could be independent and would have found a way to make it on their own at even a young age.

And as you can imagine, the Eights would not do well in common workplace settings, and more detail about the Eights in the workplace will be covered in the next section of this chapter.

Eights In The Workplace

Eights can find independence at a young age and can find a way to be financially independent. They are willing to get the more menial type of jobs when they are kids, and just starting out on their own. As much as the Eight needs to have control over anything and everyone, they are also practical which was previously mentioned. They realize that they will need to start from the bottom in order to go to the top, unlike the Seven who believes they can go at the top immediately.

And, not all Eights end up going to college. Many are actually high school dropouts as well as runaways because of clashing with authority, and they make out on their own. They will only take courses for the sake of learning and improving themselves so they can be financially independent so no one can ever have control over them at all.

That also means that once Eights are more established, then the types of career roles that are ideal for them are:

- The manager or the director of sales
- Real estate agent or developer due to their go-getting and aggressive personality
- Politician
- Marketing or advertising executive
- The head of publicity
- Freelance strategist
- Internet marketer
- Motivational speaker
- The CEO of anything

And the worst possible jobs for the Eights are:

- The average clerical 9 to 5 office job unless they are starting from the bottom

- Retail work

- Any type of job that is all about having a routine and does not have growth potential

The Eights will only start out at entry level jobs as long as there is a potential to be promoted. That also means that the high school dropouts looking for work will also have that in mind. They will take a routine-based entry-level job as long as there is a chance that they can be promoted. They will not like having to do the monotonous work and will hate even more that they will have a boss, but their practical nature causes them to give into it since they know they cannot climb to the top without starting at the bottom.

Either way, however, the Eight will find a way to be financially independent because their drive is unstoppable. And, they are frequently the multi-millionaire internet marketers who tell their stories about how they had an unstoppable drive since childhood and how they dropped out of school. They will talk about the challenges they endured and successfully conquered along the way which is how they made it to where they are currently standing.

The Eights who have it in them to be empathetic towards

others, which they all have a sentimental side that they hide unless they are reassured that their softer side will not be watered down by their need to be in control. The Challengers who fit this description are those who you do see as strong and successful motivational speakers who want to help others find it within themselves to be in control of their lives - so as long as it does not threaten their own.

They do that by telling others to inspire their stories, and even though the Eights are naturally the type to be in control, the ones who are motivational speakers teach others how to find it within themselves to be in control of their own lives.

This states right there that in some cases, Eights do relate to others, but will only agree to help others who do not pose a threat to them. That means they will only be around others willingly who they know will never be in control of them. Eights don't trust easily which was mentioned, so they still keep others at arm's length even when it comes to those who they want to inspire.

More about Eights and relationships will be covered in the next and last section of this chapter.

Eights In Relationships

Many Eights do end up alone because of the fact that they do not trust easily and are afraid to let their guard down when it comes to being intimate in any way. They fear that if they end up in relationships with others, then they will be controlled by them or the circumstances that they can bring into the relationship. This is why many Eights don't settle down and have kids either.

That is because kids control parents and the average Eight will not want to ever be in a situation that will cause them to be controlled in any way at all. However, for the Eights that do get married and have kids, they would have had to have been convinced in a strong way to get into a serious relationship at all, to begin with. Sometimes their hearts are won by those who the Eights find to be irresistible and, in those cases, as long as those who they are in a relationship with are always trustworthy, the Eights will protect them in a fierce way.

For the Eights that are open to becoming parents, they would be both fiercely protective as well as controlling. They will never allow their kids to go against their rules, but at the same time, they would go great lengths to keep their kids safe.

However, the majority of Eights do not settle down and get married because of their intense trust issues as well as their refusal to allow themselves to be controlled in any way at all. The common goal of the Eight is to be as independent as possible so they can never give any of their monetary wealth to anyone and so they can be in complete control of themselves and their situations.

In the next chapter, the last personality type of the Enneagram model will be covered. That is the Type 9 which is The Peacemaker.

Chapter 11: Type 9 - The Peacemaker

After reading the first eight personality types, you would have noticed a pattern. And the pattern would be that each of the first eight types has plenty of strong negative and self-serving traits. They are all different, and some are more extreme than others, but each and every personality type from the Enneagram model shows the negative traits are due to something they are afraid of that is in the deepest part of their core. However, the Type Nine which is the last personality type on the Enneagram model is different somewhat.

Those who are part of this type are also referred to as The Peacemakers as it is mentioned often in the late Riso's book, *Personality Types: Using the Enneagram for Self-Discovery*. And, Nines do have their challenges as well, but their overall personality is based on genuinely what they are called, which is the peace-making type.

Nines really do have the best intentions at heart and want to make sure everyone is happy, are healthy, and have their needs met. They are easy-going, trusting, faithful, charismatic and likable, reliable, and tolerant people and these traits that they have are genuine. However, Nines are far from perfect because they absolutely cannot stand conflict and will avoid any potential for it at all costs.

With that said, many Nines are introverted and do withdraw from others. However, this is not the case with all Nines. Some of them are sociable, and some of them are sociable on their own terms. Most of them do need time alone to recharge as being around too many people can be draining to them for prolonged periods of time. This may sound contradictory since they do feel connected to others, but at the same time, they don't want to be around people for too many hours in a day. This may mean they feel connected to others on a more spiritual approach. They also feel connected to the world in general on a spiritual level.

Nines also are the types to believe that things work out, even if it means that they end up working out in a different way that they had imagined. For instance, the Nine may be writing a book and has the belief that a publisher will pick up the book and accept it. However, the Nine faces a different reality and none of the publishers that he or she pitches to accept the book. However, the Nine decides to self-publish the book and ends up finding an opportunity that is relevant to the subject matter through a buyer of the book that was impressed that contacted the Peacemaker to offer an exciting opportunity.

This way, the Nine would have not had the book accepted by the publishers that he or she had pitched to but had decided to self-publish the book and attract a buyer who loved it. And the buyer loved it to the point that he or she offered the Nine an excellent opportunity that was related to the book. And things did end up working out in the end, but not in the way the Nine had imagined. And, he or she would have been at peace with it as well.

However, there are some negative traits that the Nines possess that are less serious than the other personality types. Firstly, Nines are resistant to change and prefer to keep things the way they are. But if they are forced to change in any way which at one way or another they are since life is all about evolving and changing, they do adapt much better than they give themselves credit for.

The Nines also are incredibly hard on themselves and will berate themselves for not doing something right or for hurting someone or something when they would not have been responsible for it. They also are too kind to the point that they can be easily taken advantage and taken for granted by those who prey on them. However, they still get angry. If they are angered, they will not react right away. They are the types to allow the anger to build up until they end up exploding and end up saying words that they would regret after the fact.

Some Nines will not explode if they are angry and will become passive-aggressive by dishing out the silent treatment or they can be deceptive on purpose to spite someone who did them wrong. And Nines can be grudge-holders as well which may be surprising to learn since this type would be believed to be the forgiving type.

Not all Nines are grudge-holders, as the ones who are slowly angered to the point of exploding will be likely to let it go and blow over after getting those emotions out. The Nines that are the ones that are the most likely to be grudge-holders are those who are the types to express their anger through passive-aggression.

All of the traits from the Nines would have been noticeable since early childhood. Nines as toddlers would have been like any other toddler to throw tantrums when they don't get their way because that is how they learn about themselves or their needs. However, Nines as children will be seen as affectionate, and empathetic at a young age.

As they grow and mature, and reach the age where they

start attending school, they will show this kindness to their peers, and be the type to please their teachers as well. However, as much as you would think they would stand up for the underdog or if they see a child being bullied, they would not only because they are terrified of conflict. They may, however, befriend the bully victim and spend time with him or with her privately, somewhere in the school yard away from the other kids since they need their space.

However, if the Nine as a child was seen with the victim, that would mean that the Nine would easily become a victim of bullying as well. And the Nine would run away from the bully to avoid conflict at all costs.

This also means that the Nine child would obey the parents and always follow their rules, and they would have been terrified to get into trouble. They would carry this trait throughout their personal and professional lives as well.

In the next section, Nines in the workplace will be covered.

Nines In The Workplace

Many types of jobs and career roles are a good fit for the average Nine type. The Nine would do just fine working in a typical office 9 to 5 working environment and would even be the type to pass on any promotion to others if he or she felt that the other would have been more deserving. This is how the Nines can do themselves a disservice. This type of working environment would be ideal as well because of the fact that the average Nine does not like change in any way at all and needs to be in his or her comfort zone. That is another reason that the Nine would be likely to pass up a promotion due to the fact that promotion means that they would have to meet higher expectations such as having to work overtime and having to fulfill other duties that the Nine would not be comfortable with.

The Nine would just want to keep things as they are. Go to work, then leave at 5 pm (or whatever hour it would be based on the hours he or she is working), and go home, have dinner, walk the dog, and do the nightly duties whether that involves their family or not. They would be completely content with doing this for the rest of their working years.

Sometimes, the Nine would want to make a change of some sort, but it would have to be on their own terms as they cannot handle the idea of being thrown into it. However, they do adapt better than they believe they can as it was previously mentioned. There have been many times that Nines have been fired or laid off, and they had been able to settle themselves into new jobs, especially if the jobs that they had found were similar to the ones they had previously.

Other than the predictable office 9 to 5 office job, the best jobs or career options for the Nines would be:

- Therapist
- Creative writer
- Writer in softer niches
- Creativity coach
- Human resources manager
- Social worker
- Mediator
- Teacher
- Editor
- Youth group leader
- Activist

- Any type of work with animals
- Any type of work with the disabled

The worst possible career roles or jobs for the Nines would be:

- A CEO of any company unless they have a reason to be self-employed
- Lawyer
- Banking
- Investment banking
- Financial advisor
- Anything that involves risk or being antagonizing in any way or form.

None of this would at all be surprised to learn that the Nines would be a good fit for some jobs or careers, and a poor fit for some others as it the same would apply for all personality types.

This also means that the Nines present themselves in such a way when it comes to their personal relationships which will be covered in the last section of this chapter.

Nines In Relationships

Based on what you have learned about the Nine type personality, it would not be surprising to learn that the Peacemakers make incredibly loyal partners. They would have been the types to always put the needs of others ahead of themselves. Sadly, many of them would have also been taken advantage of and taken for granted as their kindness would have been easily misused.

Nines would be the ones to be hurt easily in relationships such as being lied to or even being cheated on as well. However, the problem is that the Nines would become angry and hurt over that kind of deception. However, the Nine would also do anything to avoid conflict and end up causing the anger over being deceived into boiling up which means an explosion would end up happening. Or, the Nine would become passive-aggressive and deceive the partner as a result or do something else in a passive-aggressive way.

This also means that the Nine would have a relationship that lacks conflicts which is also not healthy, as the Nine would be building up anger and resentments for not getting his or her needs met and staying quiet about it. This means the partner would have no idea that the Nine would be upset regardless of whether the partner doing anything to intentionally upset or hurt the Nine. Communication is lacking in marriages and relationships with the Nine type which would present challenges.

The same would apply to their friendships, and the same would apply to their parenting tactics. Nines would make excellent parents because they would make sure their kids' needs are met; however, they would not be the ones to discipline them effectively because that would involve conflict otherwise. They would not want to be the cause for their kids to throw a tantrum, and unfortunately, that means their kids could become unruly due to not having enough discipline.

There needs to be balance in regard to parenting roles in that case to offset that situation.

This completes the 9 personalities of the Enneagram model, and that is not what completes the model either. There are more facets to the Enneagram as the next chapter will cover one of the other facets, which are the wings.

Chapter 12: The Enneagram Wings

There is a lot more to the Enneagram than the 9 personality types that were covered over the last 9 chapters. The personalities are just one aspect of the model, and chances are after you had read about the personality types, you had wondered if anyone really has personalities that are so extreme which were described in each of the chapters. The odds of that being the case are low because even though the personality types are what people's cores are like, they are usually watered down or influenced by other personality types.

The reasons that the personality types are colored or are influenced are because part of the Enneagram model consists of wings, which are responsible for altering the personality types as it is referenced in the late Riso's book, *Personality Types: Using the Enneagram for Self-Discovery*.

If you remember back earlier in the eBook that the personality types were compared to having a plain flavored vanilla ice cream, that in itself seems bare. The same goes for personality types. However, what you need to change it up and to flavor, it is to add toppings which could be fudge sauce, caramel sauce, or sprinkles, or nuts, whatever you choose, that is what makes the ice cream sundae more complete. The ice cream or sundae toppings are what the wings of the Enneagram model represent. The spice that is added to the core in order to make the individual more complete.

In other words, the wings are the neighboring personality types that are right next to the core type on the Enneagram model. These wings do influence your core, but they do not alter your core type just like the sundae toppings do not change the fact that the type of ice cream that they are laid over is the vanilla ice cream.

Here is a better analogy to make this clearer. Our core type is our personality type. That represents the vanilla ice cream, but if you put fudge sauce over it, then that represents the influence of one neighboring wing type. And if you put sprinkles on it, then that represents the other neighboring wing's influence on the other side.

However, in some cases, both wings are highly influential, and in other cases, one wing is more influential than the other, and that all depends on the circumstance that the individual is in. These wings are helpful and can be resourceful, and they are also there to help balance the individual as well.

Think back again to the airplane analogy. An airplane needs its wings in order to stay balanced in the air. The core by itself will not be able to do that job. The wings help keep the individual balanced as the core type by itself would not be able to maintain that type of balance at all.

The purpose of the wings is to help bring a new perspective to an individual when they are faced in any type of challenging or any type of situation. The wings also are beneficial when it comes to emotions and behavior. Let's take a look at some examples of how the wings can be beneficial to each of the 9 personalities on the Enneagram model in the next section as it will start from Type 1 to Type 4.

Type One To Type Four And Their Wings

In this section, you will learn about the first 4 types of personalities and how their types are altered by their wings when necessary:

Type 1 - The Perfectionist - The perfectionist only wants perfection and cannot stand anything that is less than perfect. The main fear that the One has is that he or she is afraid of being corrupt in any way and wants to be balanced and have integrity. The wings will help create more balance for the Ones. The Type One with a Nine wing would have influences from the Nine personality type and would provide them with a calmer approach. They still have their strong expectations, but they will be able to allow things to unfold when they rely on the Nine wing.

The Type One with a Two wing will be more of an advocate. They want perfection, and they want to help make a situation better. If a Type One goes into a homeless shelter and sees that there is abuse going on, and wants to improve things for the situation, then the One will lean on to the Two wing to advocate for the safety and better treatment of the individuals.

Type 2 - The Helper - The helper wants to please others and be there for others but has a strong possessive side. However, if Type Two relies on the One wing, then that shapes the individual for being more of a servant to others. That does not literally mean they will be maids or butlers. However, they will be the ones to deliver messages to others to make sure it is delivered properly.

Type Two with a Three wing will be the type to host events or to teach others what they have learned that can be helpful. They still want to be appreciated, and that is why those with this personality type who learn on Wing Three will be the ones to hold events or to go and teach in settings that they know that they will get their kudos for putting themselves out there.

Type 3 - The Performer - The performer is naturally charming and is only concerned about being ambitious for the sake of being the best at what they do. And they want to beat their competition as well. And, in order for them to win others over, even more, they will rely on their Two Wing in order to help others which means that they will gain what they need.

This sounds like they are strictly taking advantage of people in order for them to win, but when they rely on their Two Wing, they will genuinely help someone who is in need, but they do need to get something back from it. When the Three leans on the Four Wing, they tap into their unique side and turn it into something professional. Type Threes that are entrepreneurs have to lean towards the Four Wing in order to differentiate themselves from the competition.

Type 4 -The Romantic - This individualistic type is always looking for ways to seek out their identity because of how they fear that they have no real significance. They are quite melodramatic as well. However, the Fours that lean on their Three Wing can be unique yet have an approach to go after something which will give them confidence that they have a purpose to fulfill.

The Four that leans on the Five Wing will be more like a Bohemian, as they will realize that they are unique and will embrace it without having to make their mark. They will not throw their uniqueness in people's faces and will find a way to live comfortably with who they are on their own.

The next and final section of this chapter will focus on Type 5 to Type 9 personalities and its wings.

Type Five To Type Nine And Their Wings

In the late Riso's book, *Personality Types: Using the Enneagram for Self-Discovery* plenty of information about the personality types and their wings on the Enneagram model are covered. In the previous section, the brief descriptions of the Type One to Type Four personalities and their wings were covered. In this section, the Type Five to Type Nine personality types and their wings will be focused on before going into the next chapter which is going to be about the Enneagram centers.

However, before that is covered, let's finish this chapter by covering the wings for the Type Five to Type Nine personality types on the Enneagram model.

Type 5 - The Investigator - As you know that the Fives are quite secluded, and secretive, and they are the observers, and they spend their time gathering up information. They are not the type to make friends easily unless they find someone who they relate to and can become friends for life. In fact, their main fear is that they may end up useless and incapable. And their greatest yearning is that they are competent.

However, when the Investigator leans on the Four Wing, they become more of an iconoclastic type. They are the types that are ready to break traditions and are extremely bold thinkers. They are not afraid to rebel, and that is how they can work through their insecurities if necessary. For instance, the Five that is appalled by how a cult is brainwashing a group of people because the Five has already done research of their own to see how damaging they are can easily lean on the Four Wing in order to make a bold move by exposing the type of damage the cult has caused with proof. That will most definitely make people wake up, especially the ones who have been affected.

The Fives that learn on the other wing, which is the Six Wing end up becoming problem-solvers. The Fives are distrusting like the Sixes are, however, the Sixes are the ones that yearn to find someone or something to trust which is the biggest challenge for the Six. If the Five comes across something or someone that they are attracted to, then they can learn towards their Six Wing in order to determine how trustworthy someone is, or whether getting involved in something they are interested in is worth it. They will evaluate whether the individual or situation deserves a chance through critical thinking.

Type 6 - The Loyalist - The Loyalist is always distrusting and yearns to find something or someone to trust. They want to be committed to something or to someone and need security. However, even though they are responsible and engaging, they are extremely anxiety-ridden and suspicious. They are terrified without having support or proper guidance, and their main desire is to have the support they need as well as the security as they do not like going out of their comfort zones.

The Type Six with a Five-Wing are the types to defend others if they know they are innocent in a situation or understand their situation as to why they did something that may be unpopular. For instance, if a worn-out parent had no choice but to put their disabled child into a group home and he or she received nothing but judgment and criticism for it, then the Loyalist leaning on the Five Wing would stand up and defend the parent. Even though the

Loyalist would not understand on a personal level why the parent did what he or she needed to do, the Six would understand that the parent was burned out and could not help the child and would not hesitate to point that out to those who are judging the parent.

The Six leaning on a Seven Wing would be the type to leave their comfort zone a little and put their distrusting trait aside if they saw someone who was distraught. And, in this case, the Six would sit down next to the individual to listen to why he or she is quite upset just to give that person an ear. The Sixes are all about needing comfort and the Seven breaks the comfort zone, and in this case, the Seven Wing would help break that.

Type 7 - The Enthusiast - Sevens are adventure seekers and are naturally positive. They need to constantly have their needs fulfilled as to why they are always looking forward to the next best thing, and they are terrified of being deprived. The Sevens are not empathetic, but the Sixes are, and when the Sevens lean on their Six Wing, they want to make others happy who are having a rough time. That is why they are referred to as the entertainers, as they can easily cheer someone up who is having a bad day.

The Sevens are also not naturally practical or organized;

however, their neighboring personality type the Eight is both powerful and practical. And when the Seven realizes that he or she has to be grounded to attain a goal, then this is when he or she leans on the Eight Wing and is just as powerful but is more realistic and organized about attaining a certain goal.

Type 8 - The Challenger - Type Eight is the bold, dominating, and confident type, and will never back down if a challenge is being faced. Those who have this personality type will not back down and are the ones who must always be in charge. Their biggest yearning is that they are always in charge no matter what, and that applies to life circumstances. They are deeply afraid of being controlled or harmed by others.

However, the Eights need to lean on their wings when it comes to certain situations. And the Eight has to realize at times that he or she cannot control life's circumstances and the only way that the Eight can find acceptance is by leaning on the Seven Wing. This causes the Eight to become innovative and creative by finding a solution to be in charge of an outside circumstance that cannot be changed.

For instance, if an Eight was on a ship that was about to sink, he or she would jump off and swim over to a foreign island where he or she would not know anything about which includes the language. The Eight would find a way to learn a language and find temporary work to stay there until he or she could find a way to get back home or to the destination where he or she was heading.

And, for the Eight that needed to be in a position to protect someone else's needs, then they would lean on the Nine Wing for not just being the protector but being empathetic towards the one who needed protection. The Eight would lean on the Nine Wing to be concerned about someone else's needs other than their own if there was a situation that came up. For instance, the Eight could find a homeless individual who had been bullied. This would trigger the empathetic side in the Eight, and the Eight would then fight off the bully to help the homeless individual, and then even go and buy them a meal. That would be the result of them leaning on the Nine Wing.

Type 9 - The Peacemaker - This personality type is naturally empathetic, loyal, receptive, agreeing, complacent, and easygoing. They only want to have peace of mind, and their biggest fear is experiencing a loss. The Nine needs to lean on the Eight or One Wings in order to be in better control of their situations as well as the situations of those who they care for because without either of these wings, they will not survive with this personality type alone.

Nines that lean on the Eight Wing are referred to as the advocates. They are naturally empathetic; however, in some situations they need to be in better control of themselves or of others that are close to them. If they are in a situation where they are not getting the medical help they need for an illness they suspect they have, then they would need to lean on the Eight Wing and become bold and become their own advocates in order to receive better medical care. Or if their children were struggling in school and the teachers were not concerned, then they would be an advocate for their children to make sure that they get the type of help or education they are entitled to get. In other words, when push comes to shove, the Nine will need to rely on the Eight Wing.

And, the Nine will need to rely on the One Wing in order to turn their dream into a reality. Nines by themselves are not grounded. However, they have the ability to be, and that is when they can lean on the One Wing. The One Wing will help gain the skills and knowledge to turn their dream into something that really comes to live instead of just staying as a fantasy.

For instance, if the Nine wanted to become an author and

even become a best-seller, then the Nine would investigate what could be done to make that happen by leaning on their Perfectionist Wing.

And that concludes the Wings of the Personality Types Of The Enneagram. The examination of the Enneagram model is not finished as the next chapter will be covering the centers which are also covered in the late Riso's book, *Personality Types: Using the Enneagram for Self-Discovery*.

Chapter 13: Introduction To Centers

The onion of the Enneagram has been peeled a lot as you had already discovered it's 9 personality types, and then after learning about those, you had learned about how the personalities are tempered by their wings. And now, you are going to be learning about the centers in the Enneagram model. All of the information about the centers are derived from the late Riso's book, Personality Types: Using the Enneagram for Self-Discovery.

The 9 personality types of the Enneagram model are placed into the 3 groups which are called the centers. Each center represents the imbalances that are found in each of the personality type, which is where the negative traits of each one happens to lie. The 3 centers are the Instinctive center, the Feeling center, and the Thinking center. And each center contains the 3 personality types that share the strengths and weaknesses of that center.

Each type of personality is affected by the unconscious emotional response to not being in contact with the core in the centers. That is why the centers have negative themes. The themes of the centers are:

- **The Instinctive Center** as the One, the Nine, and the Eight personality types fall into this area, and this area represents rage and anger

- **The Feeling Center** as the Two, the Three, and the Four personality types also fall into this center, and this area represents shame

- **The Thinking Center** as the Five, the Six, the Seven personality types falls into this area as well, and this center represents fear.

After reading about the personality types more in detail, then it is not difficult to understand how these personality types could end up falling into the centers that best represent their traits. The first center that will be examined more is the Instinctive center, and the One, the Nine and the Eight personalities will be examined further as to how they are affected by the centers.

The Instinctive Center

The Instinctive center is represented by anger and rage, and it is easy to see how the Eights can be full of anger and rage but may be more difficult to understand how the Nines and the Ones are affected. Let's look further into each of the personalities that fall into this center more carefully.

The Eights affected by the Instinctive center - The Eights are all about needing to be in control, and the anger they have is instinctive, and it builds which is what strengthens their motivations. However, even with the positive side to the anger in this personality type which is put to good use. If they feel as if they are about to lose control, then rage sets in. Their rage setting in is the response to them feeling threatened by a person or a situation that could potentially have control over them.

This results in rage which causes them to easily express violence. The Eights respond to their anger in a physical way which includes them being physically violent as well as them raising their voices. Their natural, confident nature is what gives them permission to express anger in this manner. However, the Nines are fueled by anger as well as they express it differently based on their personality type.

The Nines affected by the Instinctive center - The Nines are in the same center as the Eights, and this may be difficult to believe since they are opposites personality wise. But they are equally effectively by anger and rage based on the fact that they lie in the Instinctive Center. However, whereas the Eights embrace their anger, the

Nines do not as they deny it even though they are aware it is there.

The Nines shove it away as they are not in touch with this part of them in addition to their other instincts. Nines prefer to stick to their idealizations of the world. but if they are pushed, then that anger either comes bubbling up in an explosive manner or ends up affecting them by causing them to express their anger in a passive-aggressive way. The Nines avoid their anger, and the Ones also do not embrace and express their anger the same way as the Eights do, but in a different way.

The Ones affected by the Instinctive center - The Ones are all about perfection, and if they acknowledge their angry part, they feel as if they are less than perfect which is their ultimate nightmare. This is why the Ones do what they can do repress this side to them. They do not want to ever want to be seen as angry. However, as much as they want to deny the anger, they can't. The way they channel this instinctive anger is by directing towards their inner-critic and are also quite critical of others in a way that can sting. The Eights express this anger in a violent and visible way, the Nines do to not acknowledge it, but it comes bubbling up through an explosive temper that is momentary or causes them to become passive-aggressive, and the Ones express this anger by being overly and unfairly critical of themselves and of others.

That concludes the way the Instinctive center effects personality types One, Nine, and Eight of the Enneagram model. The next center to examine is the feeling center.

The Feeling Center

The Feeling center is governed by the feeling of shame which affects personality types Two, Three, and Four. The first one to be examined is how the Twos are affected by this center.

The Twos affected by the Feeling center - The Twos are well aware of their feelings of shame and the way they suppress it is by focusing heavily on how they can be liked by others. And as long as they feel that they are appreciated, they can focus on the positive feelings they have while suppressing any feelings of shame that they may be having. And the way they want people to like them and appreciate them in a desperate way is by helping others, and this even means they would be putting their own wants and needs aside just to suppress their feelings of shame.

And, when they are threatened by someone who doesn't like them or if they do not feel appreciated, they are exposed to that shame, and this actually causes them to become angry. Their personality type is not in the Instinctive center, but shame also can bring up angry emotions which is why they are constantly feeling hysterical when they are not feeling appreciated for their efforts. The Threes also are doing what they can to suppress their feelings of shame in a different manner.

The Threes affected by the Feeling center - The Threes want to prove to themselves and to everyone else that they are winners in everything they do. They want to be the best at what is most important to them whether it is financial success or having the best-fit body. And they are constantly attempting to become the best in order to shove those uncomfortable feelings of shame which is why they are terrified of failure and feeling like they are adequate. Their extreme desire to be the best at what they do is so that they suppress their inner feelings of shame.

The positive attribute of this personality type is that this type is naturally driven even though it is for the wrong reasons. The Fours are governed by the Feeling center as well but in a much different way than the Twos and the Threes.

The Fours affected by the Feeling center - The Threes do what they can do avoid feelings of inadequacy whereas the Fours are most likely to succumb to those feelings of shame instead. However, what the Fours do in order to hide those feelings is that they show off their creativity, proudly show off their eccentricities, and make their mark about being unique as well.

Fours also are affected by feelings of shame by creating a fantasy life which causes them to escape from them having to deal with anything uncomfortable that life continuously throws at them. They do this to not only escape anything that can cause them hardships, but they do this by escaping anything that does not interest them in the least bit.

That concludes the personalities affected by the Feeling center. The last center that will be focused on is the Thinking center which effects the Five, the Six and the Seven personality types.

The Thinking Center

The Thinking center is governed by fear and the Five, the Six and the Sevens are the personalities that fall into this center, which is easily seen after learning about the nature of these personality types. The first one to be covered is how the Fives are affected.

The Fives affected by the Thinking center - The one

thing that the Fives fear the most is the external world. This is why they withdraw, are secretive and are observant, and learn what they can. They create their own inner worlds and will only allow those in it who they feel are not a threat in any way at all. Fives are seen as hermits because that is what they literally are in order to escape the outer world by keeping themselves within. They don't feel confident enough to join into the outer world, and this is based on their fear, which is why they keep to themselves.

The Sixes affected by the Thinking center - This personality type is affected by this center the most as they display plenty of anxiety over distrusting situations and people. And yet they have a strong desire to trust and have faith in others and in situations. Their fear is what prevents them from putting their distrusting and skeptical sides aside. They always find reasons to not trust someone or something even if there has been proof indicating that the individual or situation is completely Kosher.

And, Sixes will even doubt those who they have allowed them into their lives due to the fact that their fear is keeping them from being open and trusting in any way or form. They will also deal with their fear by being confrontational towards those who they do not trust which is driven by their anxiety over any situation that is causing them to be doubtful in the first place.

The Sevens affected by the Thinking center - The Fives fear the external world whereas the Sevens fear the internal world and their fear is the reason that the Sevens are constantly looking for excitement through external sources. This is the one personality type that will not be introspective in any way or form because they have to constantly look for excitement and adventure in order to escape the one thing they fear the most - and that is the inner world.

With that said, Sevens are not purposely shallow by them wanting to keep taking expensive trips and are obsessed with meeting celebrities, famous people, and people who they find to be worthy. The Sevens are not non-appreciative about the fact that they just went on an expensive trip and are looking forward to the next one each and every time. They are not purposely being thankless and taking their blessings for granted that most people would not have a chance to take even once in their lifetimes. The Sevens behave this way because they are absolutely terrified of being in their inner world and they are terrified of being trapped in it. They keep themselves engaged, busy, and occupied in many different activities at once just to escape their inner world.

That means the next time you think that someone who may be shallow for going on expensive trips all the time and not appearing to be thankful for their experiences may not be any of that at all. They may just be one of those Sevens that constantly need to escape due to the fact that they are driven by fear of being trapped. Their fear stops them from sitting down, breathing, and to smell the roses.

Bonus Chapter: Enneagram in Relationships

Using the Enneagram in Your Relationship

Love is a common subject for humans all over the world. We strive for it, can't get enough of it, sing about it, write about it, and shout about it from the rooftops. Love is good; love is great, actually. It makes us feel unstoppable, supported, and ready for anything. Two people that choose to be a team and commit to one another is a special thing, an amazing feeling, and something we all like to hold on to. Unfortunately, because we consider love to be so high on our list of needs, it can also be incredibly painful - especially when we lose it.

Ultimately, the Enneagram is a tool to help you reframe your perspective. It helps you see things about yourself and about others and brings you on a journey of self-discovery and self-improvement. When we reframe the way we look at ourselves and others, breaking it down into our motivations and not just actions or simple personality test, we are able to change and improve what happens in our lives. Using the Enneagram to reframe your perspective to improve your relationship is one of its many effective uses.

While the Enneagram is not a substitute for marriage counseling or therapy in more dire situations, it is an effective way to understand yourself and your partner. Doing so improves your relationship and opens up the opportunity for you both to grow together. In order to do all of this, you have to be working on self and you will have to have open and honest conversations with your partner. You'll find yourself reading your partner more than usual and in more depth. Don't be put off if your partner is returning the attention and reading you too; it means they are paying attention just like you, which is a positive thing.

Why Use the Enneagram in Your Relationship?

What does the Enneagram have to offer to your relationship? As already discussed, using the Enneagram for yourself will improve your relationships as a result. It's also hard not to try to type people once you dive into this. When it comes down to it, you will notice things without people telling you now that your eyes are open to it. Although it's difficult to avoid doing, it's best to have your partner type themselves rather than attempting to type them on your own. Perhaps showing them what your type is will interest them enough to take the test and read about the types to figure out their own. Knowing your partner's type will most certainly offer a great advantage for being able to overcome hurdles and anticipate their needs. There are plenty of ways the Enneagram can provide help and value to your relationship, as outlined below.

1. **Compassion and empathy**- Understanding one another is an amazing ability for any relationship. However, this can be hard to do. Using you and your partner's type, you'll be better able to come to a level of compassion and empathy for one another. This will allow for faster and more effective conflict resolution and even the avoidance of conflict altogether. When it comes down to it, one of the most important things in any relationship is respect. Respect and empathy go well together, though they aren't the same thing. You can always respect your partner, even when you do not necessarily understand them or get where they're coming from. It is respect that will help keep your relationship healthy and functioning. Respect will go a long way on its own, but if you add some genuine understanding and empathy along with it, your relationship can truly thrive. The Enneagram is an excellent tool in both cases.

2. **Conflict resolution and avoidance-** As mentioned above, the Enneagram as a whole can provide great insights into people, which aids in faster and more effective conflict resolution or avoidance. Being able to understand where your partner is coming from, what motivates them, and why something might upset them more than someone else is a unique perspective the Enneagram provides you with (it's up to you to use the knowledge you have gained). This can be as simple as knowing how much conflict upsets a type nine and what you can say or do to ease it for them. For example, if you're dealing with a type nine, instead of upsetting them

further with more confrontation, you can change the tone of the conversation, which typically will reduce conflict with this type.

3. **It can make you more humble**- We all have faults and strengths, and the Enneagram helps us identify those in ourselves. It can be hard to see these traits in ourselves otherwise, and many relationships have rocky patches because of this. When you can see where your shortcomings are, you are better able to work on them, make up for them, and embrace them, which can be extremely beneficial for a relationship. It can allow some open and honest conversations to be had which can also create more trust and understanding in a relationship. Knowing where you may be falling a little short can also help you see where some of your partner's frustrations lie and vice versa. No one is perfect; it is through self-discovery that we learn and come to terms with this and, as a result, we improve.

4. **Highlight your strengths**- Just as everyone has areas they can work on, we also all have areas we excel in. The Enneagram can help you see where your strengths are, just as they can your downfalls. You and your partner should be celebrating and using these strengths to your advantage. Celebrate each other and your wins, have fun, and connect during these positive moments.

5. **Communication**- Communication is key in any relationship. Without it, we're all just living in our own little world and guessing at everything. That sounds exhausting and not like something that anyone wants to really do. There are

many benefits to opening up the lines of communication. Everything doesn't have to be positive, but discussing even the most mundane and simple things can bring people closer together. When people can communicate effectively, they're able to thrive and work together. Having open and honest discussions without judgement allows for the sharing of feelings, fears, and desires, not just on the surface, but at the core of each of us. These kinds of conversations have incredible benefits for any relationship.

Areas of Your Relationship in Which the Enneagram Can Help

There is nothing better than knowing that someone else in this world genuinely understands you. It can be the most exciting experience to find someone who just gets you. These are the types of relationships people strive for and the ones that people think can only appear magically through sheer luck. This is not the case, though. It is something that can be learned and practiced. You have the ability to come to a great understanding for your partner - even if you are complete opposites.

There is no one you want to understand more than your partner, and who does not want that back in return? It's never too late to get a deeper understanding of the person you love. Here are three ways the Enneagram can help you strengthen your understanding:

1. **Core fears-** The Enneagram offers insights into fears

that surround a person. Often, many of our traits, motivations, and behaviors are based on the things we fear most. Knowing where your partner's fear comes from will help you understand where much of their conflict may stem from. When you can understand this, you're better able to support and comfort them, avoid conflict, and deal with conflict in more effective ways. Conflict won't stop, because it is a normal part of the human experience; however, it can be handled and dealt with in a simpler way, and it can certainly happen less. The more someone feels understood and supported, the better they will be able to cope and get back on track to integration and happiness.

2. **Motivation-** The Enneagram offers insight into people's general motivations in life, such as what they do, what they pursue, and why they pursue certain things. Knowing this about your partner is an excellent place to start. Being aware of what drives, inspires, and motivates someone to do things can help you to be more attentive and supportive of that person, and it will allow you to dig deeper. We are not talking about superficial things, here (although in some cases, that may very well be the case), but rather the deeper core desires we all have that are similar to the fears above.

3. **Emotions-** It can be hard for many people to feel vulnerable by sharing their emotions honestly, even

within a loving relationship. The Enneagram can assist in figuring out what is driving any kind of moods or mood changes. It can show us when our partners are doing well and healthy and also when they are not doing so well. Knowing this allows you to put the proper precautions and support into place. Sometimes this is hard to see in ourselves, as we may know it's happening but perhaps not why. When partners can help us be on top of this, they can start pointing it out to us in a helpful way, which is a good spot to begin.

Spiritual Relationships with the Enneagram

The Enneagram has become very popular in certain religious and spiritual circles. There's something to be said for using the Enneagram in such cases - especially as it relates to your own relationships. The Enneagram is a unique tool to develop self-awareness, and that fits well into a spiritual context

Because the Enneagram is rooted in ancient wisdom, it lends itself well to modern day spiritual people. Tools that already exist specifically for spirituality have concepts that are often difficult to grasp or their executions are too abstract.

Depending on your beliefs, the Enneagram can be used to deepen your connection with self, but it can also deepen your connection with a higher power. In this sense, it can be used to map out your spirituality or your religious motivations. Using the Enneagram to do this gives you a clearer picture of yourself and shines a light on your motives or your fears to uncover what drives you. Many beliefs out there strive for and encourage self-improvement and to be the best you can be.

In many households and relationships, spiritual beliefs are something that are fundamental to them. If this sounds like you and your relationship with spirituality, the Enneagram can also be used to strengthen the connection of your relationship to a higher power.

This is something you can do together as a couple, as well. You can introduce your spiritual beliefs however you see fit. There's room for them in this system, and there is much to be learned about yourself through the lens of your beliefs. This is why the two have become a popular pairing and definitely aid each other. If it helps you to use things like scripture to set your goals or provide you with more self-awareness, that's absolutely something that you can do within your own individual Enneagram journey and through the journey of your relationship.

Conclusion

The Enneagram or the Enneagram of Personality is a psychological phenomenon that very few people are aware of, and it stems from the Greek words ennea which means nine and gramma which means written. The Enneagram model that you had just read about in this eBook is what represents the psyche which is revealed by the 9 personality types that are interconnected.

Studies that were conducted at Iowa State University had shown the psychological beneficial effects on people after they had learned about themselves through the Enneagram. And it has been shown to have positive effects on young adults as well because after they learn about themselves through the Enneagram model, they have a much easier time accepting themselves. And this means that regardless of your age once you learn about who you are based on what the Enneagram model reveals, you have a chance to know yourself better and to find a way to heal as well.

It is unclear as to who had established the teachings of the Enneagram. It is believed that it is possible that either the late psychologist Oscar Ichazo or Claudio Naranjo had brought out the awareness of the Enneagram model. And the teachings by Naranjo may have been derived from the work that the late psychologist George Gurdjieff had done as well.

Either way regardless of who had been teaching others about the Enneagram model had created a great thing by creating the awareness about this amazing tool that can be quite healing. And at the end of the eBook, there will be an Enneagram test for you to take so you can discover your personality type. However, before getting to that, it is time to review the summary of the 9 personality types so you can refer back to it after taking the test instead of going back to the longer versions in the previous chapters on each of the personalities:

- **Type One - The Perfectionist** - The Ones are idealistic to the point that they need to get everything that they do complete in a perfect way and expect perfection from others as well. They do possess excellent self-discipline and are quite purposeful. However, they are not realistic about the fact that everything that they or anyone else can be done perfectly. And this is what frustrates them the most because perfection can never be attained which is why they have a difficult time resting.

- **Type Two - The Helper** - The Twos are extremely caring and demonstrative, and they go out of their way to help others, hence their name. However, they do these things for a catch. The catch is that they must feel as if they are adequately appreciated. If they do not feel that they are appreciated for their good deeds, then they become possessive and irrational. They will only back off if they feel they have been acknowledged for the good that they had done for others.

- **Type Three - The Performer** - The Threes are very success-driven, image-conscious, and ambitious, and will never settle for not achieving the best regardless of what is important to them. They are quite adaptive which is a good trait. However, they will go through great lengths to succeed even at the expense of others. They never accept failure.

- **Type Four - The Romantic** - This type is the individualist, withdrawn, and incredibly unique. They can be quite dramatic, temperamental, and are quite self-centered or absorbed. They also want to make themselves known, and they are quite creative and are quite expressive through their creativity. This type is seen as eccentric and as much as they don't like clones, they also deeply envy those who meet society's standards because of the fact that the Fours feel quite misunderstood.

- **Type Five - The Investigator** - The Fives are the types that are also withdrawn like the Fours, but they don't want to make themselves known in any way as they live as hermits while they observe and learn from what is going on around them. They make discoveries on their own as well. They are also quite innovative and will only socialize with those who are just like them, in private.

- **Type Six - The Loyalist** - The Sixes need their security, and they constantly want to trust something or someone, but they rarely put their guard down due to the fact that they are terrified of being hurt. Even if someone or something does not pose a threat to them at all, they will still find a reason not to trust, and they will always find a reason to remain suspicious. Even though the Sixes are incredibly anxious, they are also quite responsible.

- **Type Seven - The Enthusiast** - The Sevens are

the type to not be able to sit still and live in the moment. They will constantly look forward to the next best thing as they are never satisfied with being done with any experience that they have. This means the Sevens will be automatically booking their next trip or adventure after finishing the one they had, and it is an ongoing situation. The Sevens are not responsible and are quite scattered. However, they are quite fun loving and are the ones that will make sure someone has a good time. This personality type is all about having fun and living the high life on a consistent basis. They will never settle for the mundane and crave for freedom.

- **Type Eight - The Challenger** - The Eights are the types who demand to be in control whether or not it is of themselves, of others, or any situation they are in. They are quite decisive and practical as well. they are quite willful, domineering, self-confident and do not hesitate to be confrontational if needed. This is the most powerful personality type on the Enneagram model.

- **Type Nine - The Peacemaker** - The Nines are self-effacing as well as having a desperate need for peace as they do what they can to avoid confrontation. They are complacent and are quite easy-going. They will be the type to put their own needs last, and they are quite agreeable and receptive. The Nines are also reassuring, and they are the ones who will provide comfort to those who are needing it.

Now that you have read the summaries of the 9 personality types, there are also the wings as well as the centers of the Enneagram model that have a large influence on the personality types which were also covered previously in the eBook.

The wings of the Enneagram are the neighboring personalities that have an influence on each personality type. The wings are there to help keep those of each personality type balanced even though they will never replace the core type. And, the centers of the Enneagram model represent the imbalances that are present in the personality types.

The centers consist of 3 different groups which were covered in the previous chapter, and each center contains 3 personality types that share the traits of the center that is affecting them.

That sums up the Enneagram model which you may want

to study even in further detail. However, the one thing you will want to do in order to learn more about yourself is to take the Enneagram test so you can discover your personality type in the final chapter which is the one following this conclusion.

The Enneagram Test Where You Can Discover Your Personality

Are you ready to discover your personality type on the Enneagram model? You now have the opportunity to do so as what you will do is answer the following questions honestly in each section which will go from A to I. Then after you are finished, you will then find out your personality type after following some basic instructions after you are completed with the test. And remember, answer these questions honestly in order to get a true answer on the personality type you really are.

All you need to do is answer the questions in each section yes or no by circling the one that applies, and once you are done, you will find out your personality type after following an easy task! Let's now begin by answering the questions in section A below.

Section A

1. Are you easily motivated to succeed no matter what it takes? Yes No

2. Are you extremely focused on your appearance? Yes No

3. Do you jump at every chance you get to become the leader? Yes No

4. After you make a mistake, do you learn from it? Yes No

5. Are you naturally competitive? Yes No

6. Do you become upset if you learn that someone else has become successful in the same niche as you? Yes No

7. Do you find intimacy difficult? Yes No

8. Has anyone ever complimented you on how charismatic and charming you are? Yes No

9. Does happiness equal success in your eyes? Yes No

10. Do you consider yourself to be practical? Yes No

This concludes section A, now answer the questions asked in section B.

Section B

1. Does socializing make you uncomfortable? Yes No

2. Do you feel that you lack the inner strength to face life? Yes No

3. Does learning new things on a daily basis make you happy? Yes No

4. Are you naturally shy? Yes No

5. Do you feel if you ask others for help that you are imposing in any way? Yes No

6. Do you believe that intelligence is a gift and is beautiful? Yes No

7. Do you have a difficult time expressing your emotions? Yes No

8. Do you have a strong need for privacy often? Yes No

9. Has anyone ever told you that you seem to be generally apathetic or indifferent even though it is untrue? Yes No

10. Do you consider yourself to be an expert on the things that you are strongly interested in? Yes No

That concludes section B, now answer the yes and no question in section C honestly.

Section C

1. Do you feel like you are frequently misunderstood? Yes

No

2. Have you always believed you were different ever since childhood and did you consider yourself to be an outcast? Yes No

3. Are you naturally creative and intuitive? Yes No

4. Do you dislike others that try too hard to fit in? Yes No

5. Do you feel your life is more complicated than anyone else's? Yes No

6. Do you find yourself frequently envious of others because you perceive them as having an easier life than you? Yes No

7. Are you prone to depression, or have you been officially diagnosed with any type of depressive disorder? Yes No

8. Do you daydream often to the point that you would consider yourself to be a maladaptive daydreamer? Yes No

9. Has anyone ever told you that they thought you were quite self-absorbed? Yes No

10. Do you believe that a part of you is defective? Yes No

That concludes section C, and the questions for section D will be asked below. Be sure to circle yes or no after each question.

Section D

1. Are you upset frequently that nothing you do or that others do is 'good enough'? Yes No

2. Do you strive to make order out of chaos? Yes No

3. Are you ashamed of feeling any hint of anger? Yes No

4. Do you consider yourself to be overly serious and have a hard time finding humor in anything? Yes No

5. Do you consider yourself as frequently impatient and frustrated at yourself and at others? Yes No

6. Do you think of yourself as judgmental? Yes No

7. Do you consider yourself to be a loyal friend to your friends and a loyal partner to your partner if you are in a relationship? Yes No

8. Do you feel the need to follow the rules by the book, and do you expect others to do the same? Yes No

9. Are you extremely organized? Yes No

10. Do you think of yourself as a great leader? Yes No

That part concludes section D, and please answer the yes

and no questions honestly in section E.

Section E

1. Do you fear confrontation? Yes No

2. Do you consider yourself as an optimist? Yes No

3. Do you see the good in every situation whereas others would not? Yes No

4. Do you have an easier time adapting to new situations than you initially had thought you could? Yes No

5. Do you find yourself to be slow to anger but once you have had enough, you lose your temper? Yes No

6. Are you considerably a tolerant person? Yes No

7. Do you have an appreciation for nature to the point that you see nature as your home? Yes No

8. Do you frequently go above and beyond to help others without expecting anything in return? Yes No

9. Do you get upset when others that you care about are upset, or are you happy when others you care about are happy? Yes No

10. Do you feel you were born to be a parent or a caretaker? Yes No

That concludes section E and now answer the yes and no questions honestly in the section below, F.

Section F

1. Do you have the need to be needed by others constantly? Yes No

2. If someone is in trouble, are you the first one that is at their rescue? Yes No

3. Do you like to invite people over to your home often? Yes No

4. Do you become very upset when you feel you have been taken for granted? Yes No

5. Have you experienced burnout on a consistent basis? Yes No

6. Has anyone ever accused you of being bossy? Yes No

7. Are you in a caregiving profession such as a nurse? Yes No

8. Do you consider yourself as possessive over your loved ones? Yes No

9. If you are a parent, are you overprotective of your child or children? Yes No

10. If you are a parent of adult children, have they distanced themselves from you because you need to know every detail of their lives? Yes No

That concludes section F, and now we are onto section G, and please answer the yes and no questions honestly.

Section G

1. Do you always have the need to be in control whether it is controlling yourself, other people, as well as circumstances around you? Yes No

2. Are you highly ambitious? Yes No

3. Do you usually have a very strong appetite, and do you have a tendency to overeat without feeling any pangs of guilt? Yes No

4. Have you been able to find a way to become successfully financially independent even during trying times? Yes No

5. Do you have a hard time allowing yourself to be relaxed during intimate moments? Yes No

6. Do you avoid feeling vulnerable for any reason at all costs?

7. Do you feel you have uncontrollable anger issues, especially if you feel that someone or something is trying

to control you or if you believe you have been betrayed? Yes No

8. Are you overprotective of those who you care about the most? Yes No

9. Do you make yourself appear to be tough on the outside in order to hide any sensitive or soft spots on the inside because you do not want it seen? Yes No

10. Did you bully others when you were younger who appeared to be weaker than you? Yes No

That concludes section G, and now for the following section, H, you will need to answer the yes and no questions honestly as well.

Section H

1. Do you feel that people and anything, in general, are hard to trust? Yes No

2. If something positive happens, do you fear that the other shoe will drop because things are just simply too good to be true? Yes No

3. Do you believe that if a friend that you did once trust who had let you down still has good intentions? Yes No

4. Do you keep hoping that a pleasant situation from the

past will reappear? Yes   No

5. Do you have a need to stick to a routine because the idea of any kind of change frightens you? Yes   No

6. Do you prefer to work in a mundane office 9 to 5 job doing repetitive work or a job that is not overly stimulating over anything else? Yes No

7. if you are an adult, do you still live at home because the idea of moving away terrifies you? Yes No

8. Do you believe that if someone is unusually nice that they must have an ulterior motive? Yes   No

9. Have you been diagnosed with any type of anxiety disorder or do you suspect you have one? Yes No

10. Did you suffer from intense separation anxiety when you were a child that took you a long time to overcome? Yes   No

Now that concludes section H, and now onto the final section of this test, section I. Please answer the yes and no questions as honestly as you can.

Section I

1. Do you have a hard time staying in the moment? Yes No

2. Are you overly excited about the next possible thing that could come up? Yes No

3. Are you usually extroverted to the point that you despise being on your own? Yes No

4. Were you one of the popular kids when you were in school? Yes No

5. Are you spontaneous to the point that you would run somewhere if you felt you needed to even before finishing a meal? Yes No

6. Do you have a difficult time sitting still or slowing down? Yes No

7. Do you have a great desire to meet a celebrity or have you gone through great lengths to meet a celebrity? Yes No

8. Do you consider yourself to be fun, and do people flock to you for that reason? Yes No

9. Do you consider yourself to be a master multi-tasker? Yes No

10. Have you suffered from additions of any kind? Yes No

That concludes the Enneagram test where you can discover your personality.

The next thing you need to do in order to find out what your personality type is to go through each of the sections you had filled out from A to I and add up the highest amount of questions where you had answered Yes.

After doing that, you can go in the next section where the answers are and make the determination of where your personality falls on the Enneagram model.

Your Personality Type Can Be Found Right Here

Now you have the answers to the questions you had answered while you had taken the test. And if you had answered Yes to most of the questions asked in each of the sections, your personality type will be revealed which you will find below:

if you answered Yes to most of the questions in Section A, then fall into the Type 3- The Performer personality.

If you had answered Yes to most of the questions in Section B, then you are in the.

Type 5 - The Investigator group.

If you had answered Yes to most of the questions asked in Section C, then you fall into the Type 4 - The Romantic personality group.

If you had answered Yes to most of the questions asked in Section D, then you most definitely fall into the Type 1 - The Perfectionist group.

If you had answered Yes to most of the questions in Section E, then you are in Type 9 - The Peacemaker group.

If you had answered Yes to most of the questions asked in Section F, then you are in Type 2 - The Helper group.

If you had answered Yes to most of the questions asked in Section G, then you are in Type 8 - The Challenger group.

If you said Yes to most of the questions asked in section H, then you fall into the Type 6 - The Loyalist group.

If you said Yes to most of the questions asked in section I, then you fall into the Type 7 - The Enthusiast group.

And the last question that will be asked is once you have made this discovery, does it resonate with you? And since this is quite eye-opening, what more can you learn about yourself? Finding out your Enneagram personality type will now provide you the doorway to the healing that you will benefit from if you are open to that. Either way, you now know more about yourself than you did before reading this eBook.

References

Baron, R., & Wagele, E. (1994). *Enneagram Made Easy: Discover the 9 Types of People*. HarperSanFrancisco.

Ichazo, O. (1982). *Interviews with Oscar Ichazo*. New York: Arica Institute Press.

Naranjo, C. M. (1994). *Character and neurosis - an integrative view*. Gateways Books & Tapes,us.

Riso, D. R., & Hudson, R. (1996). *Personality types: Using the Enneagram for self-discovery*. Boston: Houghton Mifflin.

Book - II

Enneagram in Relationships

Understand Your Personality Type and Other Personalities to Build Healthy Relationships

Introduction

Marriage isn't the end-point of a relationship. It's just a stepping stone, one aspect of a long-term evolution between two people who have, for whatever reason, decided to take a leap of faith and say, 'Well, hey, this is a person who I want to try with for the rest of my life.' Which is not a guarantee of perfection - far from it. - Marjorie Liu

Are you tired of trying to figure out how to read your partner? Imagine finally being able to get on the same page as your loved one. How would that change your relationship or your life as a whole? Take a moment to consider how having a deeper understanding of yourself can impact your well-being, self-esteem, and relationships. Feeling stuck in one place in a relationship can be incredibly frustrating. It's not a point anyone wants to be at in a relationship with someone they love and care about deeply. As humans, we are social animals and often strive for meaningful and long-lasting relationships. In order for a relationship to reach your goals, they need to be healthy goals. Reaching these types of goals are often easier said than done, but being able to understand yourself and your partner on a deeper level is an important step towards doing so successfully.

Welcome to the world of Enneagrams and self-discovery. With the help of this book, you'll be able to understand you and your partner's personality types, which will aid you in finding out who you really are at the core and help you to understand your partner's personality, which will strengthen your relationship and help you perceive who your partner is on a completely different level. When partners empathize with each other and have a true understanding of each other's personality type, the relationship thrives. Not only is typing your partner an effective way to build on your relationship, but it is also a powerful way to navigate the other relationships in your life.

As a more holistic approach to personality types and self-discovery, the Enneagram lends itself useful to not only understanding oneself, but others as well. When we can type and understand who we have relationships with, we can easily improve those connections with others. After all, being able to understand your partner and vice versa is an integral part in any relationship.

At first glance, an Enneagram may look intimidating, but once you understand the basics, which we will go over shortly, they are quite fascinating and much easier to comprehend than it may seem. The Enneagram is a useful tool on your journey of self-discovery that will allow you to dig deeper and more honestly than you ever have before. Through this simple guide, you'll be able to type yourself and get a better understanding of what that means, not only for you, but also for the people around you. You will learn tips, get real life examples, and practice exercises to help you on your path. The Enneagram can quickly show you what might normally take many years of dedication to mindfulness practice and self-exploration to find out, and it can do so in a more unique and accessible way.

Just as we all accept and show love in specific ways, we have similar tendencies, traits, and preferences when it comes to everything else. Being open to understanding this about yourself and others will enable you to create deeper, fuller, and healthier connections with yourself and the people around you. You may also find that you'll know who to avoid or how to deal with types that you may have trouble with. The Enneagram is a way to understand what motivates people and the reasons for their behavior, values, the way they think, and the way they problem solve. This is critical information when you're attempting to be more empathic and connected to others.

Terri L. Orbuch, a well-known and respected psychologist that has devoted her career to relationships, says that small changes in behavior and attitude over time are what creates happiness in marriages and relationships (Orbuch, 2015). The Enneagram is an effective tool to aid you on this journey. Through the use of typing and being able to understand your partner's needs based on personality, you will be better able to implement other tools. Knowing your partner well and being able to empathize and understand how they work at their core are ways to effectively implement changes in your behavior and attitude to positively impact your relationship. Starting with yourself is where the journey begins; at the base of everything you do and every relationship you have is you. With that being said, relationships are partnerships, and if you are using this book to gain a better understanding of how you can improve your partnerships, it would be helpful for your partner to do the same. The better each partner understands one another, the more open the lines of communication, trust, and ultimately a deeper connection will be.

Chapter 1 : Enneagram, Its Origins and Types

Personality has been a subject of interest to scientists for many years. It is a part of a question it seems everyone asks at least once in their life: What makes us who we are? In other words, what exactly makes us human? Philosophers and scientists alike have pondered this question, many of them coming up with various theories and answers for it. It was Hippocrates in 400 BC who suggested that there exist four types of temperaments, or personalities, of people (Merenda, 1987). We have come a long way since the father of Western medicine suggested these four types. His theory is one that has led to how we look at personality today. As psychologists continue to study the way our minds work and how we behave, the Enneagram has allowed us to look within ourselves for many of these answers already. The enneagram symbol has an interesting and somewhat mysterious lineage, though it was used throughout history as symbol of self-renewal.

An enneagram is a nine-sided figure used to represent nine different personality types and the ways they interact with each other. The illustration of one may be confusing at first glance, but the further you dive into the subject of enneagrams, the more you will get out of it. To break it down further, an enneagram is a circle with the numbers one through nine placed around it, with nine being at the top. Each number represents a personality type. Inside the circle, you'll notice lines. These lines show the ways energy moves, depicting significant information surrounding our psychological patterns. The Enneagram personality types look at both directions one can go in health; integration (the healthier you are) and disintegration (your lower points of health) focuses on you as a whole. This can be a useful tool in understanding oneself and to take caution in weaknesses and the paths you may take. They represent how personalities intertwine and move around. While we always have our basic personality type, we also share traits from other ones, and the Enneagram can show the paths each personality may follow (O'Hanrahan, n.d.). The nine personality types come from three groupings of three types each. The larger triad is the basis behind the smaller personality groupings, including feeling, thinking, and instinctive. You can look at the Enneagram on many different levels. How deep you go is up to you. One way to look at it is to perceive each type as an expression of the larger triad (feeling, thinking, and instinct).

To learn about the enneagram, it's helpful to understand some important points about its background. The origins of the enneagram symbol are debated among people who study it. Some put its origins at the tenth and eleventh centuries respectively, and others speculate that it originates in the middle east or Babylon around 2500 B.C. Even in its known locations in these earlier times, it was always used as a tool or symbol for self-renewal and self-discovery.

Oscar Ichazo is known for his modern take on the enneagram. It is thought that, as the name enneagram suggests, a Greek lineage is also at play. With its links to math through ratio, geometry, and proportion, as well as its purpose for self-renewal, this is a theory that Ichazo supports. The enneagram would eventually make its way into the western part of the world thanks to George Ivanovich Gurdjieff, a spiritual teacher and adventurer who transformed it into what we know today (Riso & Hudson, 1996).

While its early beginnings may not be so clear, the enneagram has strong roots in recent Western society. The Enneagram of personality types that we know today is a combination of many ancient teachings put together to create the modern version of the Enneagram, which is based on the knowledge of Oscar Ichazo. Born in Bolivia, Ichazo traveled to Buenos Aires to learn at a school about inner workings. He later traveled throughout Asia, where he was able to gather more information and gain additional knowledge. Afterwards, he then went back to South America to develop what he had learned through his schooling and travels.

His work led him to create the Arica School to pass on what he had learned to others. Thus, the traditional modern Enneagram as we know it by Ichazo is from the 1960s. The Enneagram and, in turn, Ichazo's teachings, include aspects from many beliefs from our history (Christianity, Taoism, Islam, Judaism and Greek philosophy, to name a few). Through the Arica School, American psychologists began to study before Ichazo permanently moved to the US. It was through these people and his move that the Enneagram system and teachings made their way through North America ("Traditional Enneagram (History) — The Enneagram Institute", n.d.).

How to Use the Enneagram

Once you have gotten a good sense of the figure itself, you can find out your Enneagram type through testing. In the next chapter, you will get the chance to do so. Once you have your type, you will be able to read about it and compare it to others. Looking at the Enneagram will help the symbol make more sense, and it will allow you to dig deeper into the meaning. For example, you'll see the lines branching off from your number, with one line being integration, which is your growth, and the other being disintegration. The disintegration line is a path you may take under stress.

For example, if an average or unhealthy type eight is under pressure, the individual may act like an unhealthy or average type five. The opposite is true for the integration line. You'll also be able to discover which triad your type falls into, and this will also provide you with insight. The numbers directly to the left and right beside your type may be a subtype. We all have only one base personality type, but we can also have subtypes, and those subtypes play an important role for us, too.

Once you are able to find this information, what can you do with it? Understanding yourself and others should make you happier as a person. It provides you with insight into others that makes you better able to read and understand them. For example, things that may seem superficial or unimportant to you may be a core issue for someone else. Allowing yourself to be open, perceptive, and knowledgeable about people's personalities and types can help avoid potential problems and assist in solving them with more ease and understanding when they arise.

On the other side of this, it's integral for you to know yourself and to be honest with yourself about your strengths, weaknesses, fears, needs, desires, and shortcomings. If you are avoiding viewing yourself honestly and critically as you do others, you will not grow. You'll have trouble changing, and you won't be moving forward towards your greater potential. You'll also be preventing yourself from making better, stronger, longer lasting, and more important connections with people in your life. It's through knowing yourself that you can discover what you want and how to get there, whether it is purely out of desire for self-improvement and discovery or through the lens of your relationships.

Benefits of the Enneagram

There are many benefits to using the Enneagram. For understanding people's behavior, motivations, thinking, and ways of solving problems, it is a great resource. With a long history in our world, the Enneagram combines the wisdom of the ancients with more modern concepts. The

Enneagram can be used for anything, and people often end up using it in every aspect of their lives - from it's more conventional use as an effective personality assessment to its applications for things like relationships, deeper studies into psychology, and even your finances.

The Enneagram helps you answer fundamental questions about yourself: What are my strengths and weaknesses? What do I need to be cautious of? What do I need more of in my life? As a tool for self-discovery, there are many more uses for it, and it also has a lot of positive impacts the more you dive in. It increases your understanding of self, self confidence, and self-esteem, it makes you aware of what you need to be cautious of, and it helps you break down and evaluate your behaviors and motivations.

The Enneagram system helps you increase your capacity and the effectiveness of positive thinking as well as aiding in letting go of emotional issues that cause you to fall into distress. It allows you to focus on what is happening and why and to focus on your emotions and situations that affect your behavior and patterns. During your journey, you may find that you are less judgmental and critical of yourself and others. Through your understanding of self, a sense of renewed purpose and strength can be delivered to you.

The Enneagram is helpful in supporting you through transitions in your life by making you more mindful and aware of your tendencies, fears, and motivations. You can use it to find what it is you want in your life and to discover what path you are headed on.

In your everyday life, knowing about the Enneagram personality types can help you understand your friends, families, and coworkers. It can provide parents with insights into their relationships with their children and together as a family unit. It can also help them become better parents and increase their compassion and understanding during difficult times. Additionally, it can be a useful tool for people who manage staff to effectively avoid confrontation and de-escalate any problems that may arise. In a workplace, the Enneagram personality types can be a useful way to create groups of employees that will result in more production and efficiency.

In your romantic relationships, the Enneagram can help you understand, empathize with, and relate to your partner, and it can aid in effective conflict resolution or at preventing conflict. It's an effective way to understand your partner's motivations, fears, strengths, and behaviors. It's also a great opportunity to go on a journey of not only self discovery, but also of discovery of your partner and your relationship as a whole.

You may find yourself becoming more accepting of yourself and others and forming a deepened sense of self compassion, as well as compassion for your relationships. On a path of discovery, the learning opportunities and the benefits are endless. You won't end up on the same path as everyone else, and what you discover is yours alone to know and benefit from. There is much to be said for embracing the system and allowing you to immerse yourself in as much or as little as you wish. If nothing else, the Enneagram of personality types is an interesting look at the people around you and a fun way to view yourself.

With its growing popularity, the future of the Enneagram is bright. Many teachers offer to help people understand the system along their voyage of self-discovery. There is something to be said for everyone being mindful of what their type is. It's a system that can go beyond what it is now as it develops and grows.

Quick Overview of the Types and Triads

As you continue on your discoveries of the Enneagram, it's important to have a base understanding of what it entails. Below is a summarized list of the types, their disintegration and integration directions, and their triads for your referencing purposes while looking at the Enneagram. You can find descriptions for each type in chapter four.

While looking at the types, please note that no type is inherently feminine or masculine and that they apply equally to all genders. Not everything listed in your type may apply to you in the moment; you are constantly influx, changing between healthy, average, and unhealthy traits depending on your life and circumstances (The Enneagram Institute", n.d.). You only have one base type that is set in childhood, and you may also find parts of yourself in the other types, which is completely normal. Your base type does not change, but you may find that your traits within the type change with the circumstances. You may also find you have a dominant subtype or wing. This is typically one of the numbers beside your base type. For example, if your base type is three, your wing or subtype may be a two or four.

Feeling triad: Two, three, four

Thinking triad: Five, six, seven

Instinctive triad: Eight, nine, one

Type One: This is the reformer, instinctive triad. Type one's integration line leads to seven, and the disintegration line leads to four.

Type Two: This is the helper, feeling triad. Type two's integration leads to four, and the disintegration line leads to eight.

Type Three: This type is the motivator, feeling triad. Type three's integration line leads to six, and the disintegration line leads to nine.

Type Four: This is the individualist, feeling triad. Type four's integration line is one, and the disintegration line leads to two.

Type Five: This type is the investigator, thinking triad. Type five's integration line leads to eight, and the disintegration leads to seven.

Type Six: Type six is the loyalist, thinking triad. Type six's integration line is nine, and the disintegration line leads to three.

Type Seven: This is the enthusiast, thinking triad. Type seven's integration line is five, and the disintegration line leads to one.

Type Eight: The leader, instinctive triad is type eight. Type eight's integration line is two, and the disintegration line leads to five.

Type Nine: Type nine is the peacemaker, instinctive triad. Type nine's integration line is three, and the disintegration line leads to six.

Chapter 2 : Enneagram Test

Knowing which type you are is an important step in your self-discovery journey with the Enneagram. Below is a test to aid you in your typing. As you answer the questions in each section, keep track of each answer. When you have completed the test, score the sections individually. To find your score, you'll need to add up the values of all your answers within each section, which will have its own score. Ideally, your highest score will be your type. Once you know which section has the highest score, you can read more about the types after the test in the next chapter.

It's best to read through all of the types to see which ones resonate with you the most. Doing this is often an effective way to determine your type, and it's also a good way to determine between types when you receive more than one type with close scores on the test. You may find parts of yourself in many of the types, but you have only one base type.

As you answer the questions, keep yourself open, and answer them honestly. Your first instinct when answering is usually correct; it can be best to avoid putting too much thought into each answer for this reason. The more honest you are with yourself, the more accurate your score will be. Keep in mind that no one type is better than another, and the number of sections or types do not hold importance over any other. All types have positive and negative traits. Take a moment to clear your mind, find a quiet spot, consider each question, and answer honestly.

The Test

Each question is scored on a scale from 1 to 5. You would score a statement at a 1 if you strongly disagree with it and at a 5 if you agree with it completely. The higher the score on a section, the more closely you match with that particular type.

Section One

1. I have a strong sense of right and wrong.

1   2   3   4   5

2. I'm a perfectionist.

1   2   3   4   5

3. I consider myself to have high standards that I abide by.

1   2   3   4   5

4. I don't want to be wrong.

1   2   3   4   5

5. I put much of my focus on improving.

1   2   3   4   5

6. My inner critic is hard to ignore.

1   2   3   4   5

7. I strongly disapprove when I feel something is unjust.

1   2   3   4   5

8. Responsibilities are critical to follow through with.

1   2   3   4   5

9. I feel as though if I don't embody good, than I'm not worthy.

1   2   3   4   5

10. It's hard for me to let go of control.

1   2   3   4   5

Section Two

1. I have a strong desire to help others.

1   2   3   4   5

2. I go above and beyond for people, even when I should not.

1   2   3   4   5

3. I have difficulty setting and maintaining personal boundaries.

1   2   3   4   5

4. I'm good at anticipating the needs of others.

1   2   3   4   5

5. My self-esteem lowers when I do not get approval from others.

1   2   3   4   5

6. I take on the emotions and stress of those around me.

1   2   3   4   5

7. I find myself changing in order to fit in with others.

1   2   3   4   5

8. I have difficulty focusing on self-care.

1   2   3   4   5

9. One of my driving forces is to be loved.

1   2   3   4   5

10. One of my biggest fears is not being worthy of love.

1   2   3   4   5

Section Three

1. I have great potential.

1   2   3   4   5

2. I'm ambitious and go for what I want.

1   2   3   4   5

3. I thrive on external praise for my achievements.

1   2   3   4   5

4. I often overwork myself or take on too much.

1   2   3   4   5

5. My physical image is important to me.

1   2   3   4   5

6. I am very competitive and thrive on competition.

1   2   3   4   5

7. I need everything to be efficient and run efficiently.

1   2   3   4   5

8. It's unacceptable for others to get in the way of my momentum.

1   2   3   4   5

9. I'm adaptable in the face of challenges.

1   2   3   4   5

10. One of my driving forces is to be valuable.

1   2   3   4   5

Section Four

1. I feel the need to fill my life with beauty.

1   2   3   4   5

2. I need creative activities or hobbies.

1   2   3   4   5

3. I fear not being significant to myself and others.

1   2   3   4   5

4. My emotions run particularly deep.

1   2   3   4   5

5. I am honest with myself about my emotions.

1   2   3   4   5

6. Self-pity is one of my biggest downfalls.

1   2   3   4   5

7. I'm acutely aware of my differences from others.

1   2   3   4   5

8. Expressing myself is an important aspect of who I am.

1   2   3   4   5

9. I withdraw from others during times of uncertainty or melancholy.

1   2   3   4   5

10. I look for depth and meaning in all of my relationships.

1   2   3   4   5

Section Five

1. I have a profound need to know how and why things work.

1   2   3   4   5

2. I prefer to work and spend much of my time alone.

1   2   3   4   5

3. I find myself analyzing everything I can.

1   2   3   4   5

4. Feelings are difficult for me to process and express.

1   2   3   4   5

5. I consider myself to be very perceptive.

1   2   3   4   5

6. One of my biggest fears is being helpless or useless.

1   2   3   4   5

7. I thrive with complex ideas.

1   2   3   4   5

8. I consider myself to be quite skilled in one or more specialty areas.

1   2   3   4   5

9. Being self-reliant is especially important to me.

1   2   3   4   5

10. I do not depend on social validity.

1   2   3   4   5

Section Six

1. I consider myself to be someone that steers towards commitment.

1   2   3   4   5

2. Loyalty is very important to me.

1   2   3   4   5

3. One of my biggest fears is being without support.

1   2   3   4   5

4. I'm a particularly good problem solver.

1   2   3   4   5

5. I'm able to foresee problems before they arise and plan for them.

1   2   3   4   5

6. I would say I'm a particularly skeptical person.

1   2   3   4   5

7. Stress and anxiety are problems for me when I'm not at my best.

1   2   3   4   5

8. Being secure in my life and all aspects of it is important to me.

1   2   3   4   5

9. My thinking is often different from or more radical than my peers.

1   2   3   4   5

10. I would describe myself as a strategic thinker.

1   2   3   4   5

Section Seven

1. I consider myself to be adventurous.

1   2   3   4   5

2. I crave variety in my life and activities.

1   2   3   4   5

3. I am not particularly concerned with people's opinions of me.

1   2   3   4   5

4. I am a fairly happy and positive person.

1   2   3   4   5

5. I am known to be too impulsive.

1   2   3   4   5

6. I fear missing out on new or exciting things.

1   2   3   4   5

7. One of my biggest fears is not living a worthwhile life.

1   2   3   4   5

8. I consider myself to be a forward-mover.

1   2   3   4   5

9. I tend to not want to be as committed as my peers to things or people.

1   2   3   4   5

10. One of my biggest fears is to feel deprived.

1   2   3   4   5

Section Eight

1. I consider myself to be someone who needs to be in control of everything.

1   2   3   4   5

2. I particularly enjoy challenges for myself and challenging others.

1   2   3   4   5

3. I get angry easily and have a temper.

1   2   3   4   5

4. One of my biggest fears is being controlled by someone else.

1   2   3   4   5

5. Weakness is unacceptable to me.

1   2   3   4   5

6. Being self-reliant is incredibly important to me.

1   2   3   4   5

7. I tend to take on the leadership role in groups or situations.

1   2   3   4   5

8. I have trouble admitting my feelings of vulnerability to myself and others.

1   2   3   4   5

9. I have a high enthusiastic drive to accomplish tasks and goals.

1   2   3   4   5

10. I have trouble and get impatient with typical social rules and constructs.

1   2   3   4   5

Section Nine

1. I don't like or partake in arguments or confrontation.

1   2   3   4   5

2. I consider myself to be a person who likes to keep everything harmonious.

1   2   3   4   5

3. I consider myself to be particularly open and accepting of others.

1   2   3   4   5

4. Making decisions is difficult for me, because I see many points of views.

1   2   3   4   5

5. Negative situations and feelings are troubling for me, so I avoid them.

1   2   3   4   5

6. I have trouble finding my own strong sense of identity.

1   2   3   4   5

7. I am likely to put others before myself more often than not.

1   2   3   4   5

8. In a situation of conflict, I am likely the person to initiate peace.

1   2   3   4   5

9. One of my biggest fears is of loss.

1   2   3   4   5

10. Finding balance within myself and in my environment is very important to me.

Enneagram 2 manuscripts in 1

1   2   3   4   5

Chapter 3 : The Types

Below you will find a description for each personality type within the Enneagram. While reading, please keep in mind that the number for each type does not indicate any significance or more importance over others. The types are universal, meaning that they don't discriminate and include all genders, ages, races, etc. All of the types have positive and negative traits, and they all take on healthy and unhealthy traits from other types at their best and worst.

There will likely be one or two types that stand out to you the most. One of these is often your base type and possibly your subtype. Only you can truly tell what your type is, because you know yourself best. While having an understanding of the Enneagram is helpful in dealing with other people, it's only a guess, as the same thing applies to everyone.

Type One

The type one is known as the reformer. These individuals are always striving to improve; they're the perfectionists of the feeling triad. Also, they harbor a strong moral sense. Their conscious tells them right from wrong, and they stick to that with great strength. This makes them amazing advocates and teachers, which are roles they often take on.

Ones have a fear of being incorrect or morally wrong, which is seen in many of their driving forces and strengths. Perfectionists hold high standards and do not take well to failure. Being a part of the bigger instinctive triad, they can be found using their instincts to their advantage.

If you're a one, you may perceive yourself as someone who fights for positive change, has idealist views, holds high standards for yourself, and has a strong sense of right and wrong (and wanting to be seen this way by others).

The strong drive that appears in ones puts them on a mission to be useful. They do care about the criticisms of others and strive to ensure they get positive outcomes because of this.

Moving towards disintegration for ones, methodical individuals of this type can become moody and irrational, shifting to a type four. With the one's direction of integration (growth), critical and angry people of this type become more joyful on the path to a healthy seven ("Type Descriptions — The Enneagram Institute", n.d.).

Type Two

Type twos are the helpers and the people pleasers. They live to be useful to others, so they are generally friendly, generous, warm, and empathetic people. As a member of the feeling triad, they have a strong driving desire to be loved and liked.

Twos care very much about what others think of them and are open with their feelings. These traits make them great in delicate situations or in jobs that require a lot of empathy. They are compassionate, caring, and nurturing to the people and things in their lives.

If you are a two, you may find that you're the type of person that puts everyone before yourself. There are likely countless times you've gone out of your way to go above and beyond for someone else.

Moving along the path of direction of disintegration (stress), the more needy twos become aggressive like a type eight. When moving in the direction of integration (growth), prideful twos become more self-nurturing and emotionally capable ("Type Descriptions — The Enneagram Institute", n.d.).

Type Three

This type is the achiever. Type threes are driven and drawn to success. Their main motivation for this is being successful. Threes can be particularly charming and are known for their ambition. Their drive and need for success is usually rightfully placed as a well-versed, confident, and competent people.

Threes are often the people who are viewed as workaholics. Their drive to achieve and do well in life is so demanding that work can overtake them. This can come from both positive and negative places and lead to corresponding outcomes. Not surprisingly, threes are among the most competitive people.

Behind that driving force, threes are concerned with their image and how others perceive them. With success comes admiration, but there's also a separation of self from others. Simply put, threes like to stand out, and they want recognition for it.

When normally driven, threes head towards disintegration, and they follow the line to nine and becoming disengaged. Following their line of integration, threes that may be arrogant, too vain, or dishonest find themselves as a healthier six, at which point they are helpful, committed, and cooperative with others ("Type Descriptions — The Enneagram Institute", n.d.).

Type Four

The type four is the individualist. These types of people are highly creative and are likely drawn to activities and hobbies in the arts. They have a need to explore expression, whether it be creatively or through emotion. Through their creativity, fours try to make their own identity. Identity is important to fours because of this. They want to set themselves apart from others and show and support their individuality. Their identity is important to them, so they want to create and mold one.

Fours feel as though they are different from other people at their core. They are are often reserved and sensitive and like to withdraw themselves for this reason. They shy away when they feel vulnerable and self-conscious. They can feel like they're not included or even exempt from the world and what others would consider normal living by their own standards. Above all else, their emotional state takes precedence. Fours strive to maintain an emotional and mental balance where they normally have trouble doing so.

When fours are heading towards disintegration, they follow the line to two, becoming overly involved. Following their line of integration, fours that are emotionally chaotic find themselves at a healthier one where they are more stable and principled ("Type Descriptions — The Enneagram Institute", n.d.).

Type Five

The investigator is the type five. Fives can be fairly intense people. They are also very perceptive and innovative, thriving with complex thinking and challenges. Their curiosity drives much of their thought, and you will often find fives on the forefront of new thoughts about our world and environment. They want to know how and why things work the way they do.

Knowledge and learning is important for fives as they fear being useless and helpless. Fives easily become detached from people and their surroundings and can often be lost in thought, and this is something that others can find hard to understand. It's easy for a five to set themselves apart from others, as they like being isolated.

Often, the need of fives to gain knowledge can come from a place of insecurity, because they find much of their self-esteem within their minds and what they know. You may find fives always have a question they're asking, not necessarily to anyone else, but rather one they are figuring out and pondering themselves.

When fives are heading towards disintegration, they follow the line to seven, becoming scatterbrained and overly active. Following their line of integration, fives find themselves at a healthier eight where they're more decisive and confident ("Type Descriptions — The Enneagram Institute", n.d.).

Type Six

Type six is the loyalist. They are a committed and hard-working people, and like the name suggests, they're loyal in this sense. This stems from their desire for guidance, support, and security in their lives and with the people around them.

Sixes are wonderful problem solvers and can be known to take on a lot of responsibility. They are often thought of as creatures of habit. This can lead them to be quite anxious, defensive, high-strung, and reactive. Although sixes are among a very trustworthy group, because of this, it is also important to show loyalty to them in return. Their beliefs are strong and, being true to their loyalty, they'll fight for them with everything they have.

When sixes are heading towards disintegration, they follow the line to three, becoming competitive and too arrogant. Following their line of integration, sixes find themselves at a healthier nine where they are more relaxed and positive ("Type Descriptions — The Enneagram Institute", n.d.).

Type Seven

This type is the enthusiast. Sevens are highly energetic and spirited people. They can be bubbly, positive, and optimistic; they're great fun to have around you.

Sevens thrive on variety, so the same old thing all the time doesn't cut it for them. They love to be spontaneous, but they're also a very practical group, which aids them in their search for variety. Sevens can be unpredictable and seek constant new experiences in their lives.

You may find that sevens are also a bit distracted and impulsive. Much of their need for experiences comes from a fear of not having opportunity, not having enough, being deprived in some way, and being incapable or in pain. It's important for sevens to be able to seek their adventures, often needing their freedom to support this happiness in their lives.

When a project, hobby, or activity catches a seven's attention, they're immediately enthusiastic about it. Type sevens are part of the thinking triad. Sevens may be among the more scatterbrained, but they are practical people with the capability to come up with answers and solve problems fast and effectively. They often have more than one thing going on at any given time, and they're able to juggle it all.

When sevens are heading towards disintegration, they follow the line to one, becoming too critical and take on a perfectionist persona. Following their line of integration, sevens find themselves as a healthier five where they're more focused ("Type Descriptions — The Enneagram Institute", n.d.).

Type Eight

The challenger is the type eight. People of this type are a dominant and assertive group in all areas of their lives. They like to be in control and are not afraid of confrontation. They're perceived as being strong and to the point and the ones to go to for making decisions.

Eights can be intimidating and have a problem with their temper. This stems from a fear of not being in control or being harmed by others. It's important for eights to be in control of situations and to be self-reliant.

Eights want to show the world what they've got. They want to stand out and be known for what they do and for their strengths. You'll likely find eights in charge and leading whatever situation they're in and people they're around. Keeping their power for as long as possible and doing something with it is important to eights.

When normally confident eights are heading towards disintegration, they follow the line to five, becoming fearful. Following their line of integration, eights find themselves at a healthier two where they are more caring ("Type Descriptions — The Enneagram Institute", n.d.).

Type Nine

Type nine is the peacemaker. Nines like their lives and situations to be stable and run smoothly. Confrontation is not something they like to deal with. Quite like the mediator they tend to be, nines will go with the flow of others to keep the peace.

Nines will often downplay negative issues or other's feelings because of their strong aversion to conflict. They can be wonderful people to have around, as they are often trusting, honest, and positive. They are embracing and accepting as well, staying true to their type. Nines like stability in all aspects of their lives, and they crave balance.

Often creative and fun, nines tend to prefer being around people. They have a fear of being separated from others, because they need people to balance out their lives. They desire connections to others and strive to keep the peace for not only the people in their lives, but most importantly, in their own life. Upsetting things are not something that nines deal well with in their lives, often minimizing or shying away from anything of the sort. Peace and harmony are important to nines; this is what they strive for. Nines can be stubborn and set in certain ways, but complacent while attempting to keep the peace.

When complacent nines are heading towards disintegration, they follow the line to six, becoming more anxious. Following their line of integration, neglecting nines find themselves at a healthier three, where they are more apt to develop self ("Type Descriptions — The Enneagram Institute", n.d.).

Chapter 4 : Enneagram as a Self-Discovery and Introspection Tool

The Enneagram is a powerful tool for self-discovery, introspection, and self-improvement. People often have the misconception that the Enneagram is a simple personality test that doesn't provide the user with much value other than entertainment. So, what makes it different than any other random personality test we can take online? While it is a tool to discover your personality type yourself, there is much more value taken from typing yourself than mere entertainment. When you're able to accurately find your Enneagram type, you start down a journey of self-reflection and self-improvement.

The Enneagram offers as much depth as you desire; it really all depends on you. Perhaps taking the test and typing yourself is enough to tell you what you need to know, and that's that. Perhaps at this point in your life, you do not feel the need to look any farther. For some people, this is the case, and that's perfectly okay. For many others, the step into the Enneagram is one into an environment of being honest with themselves.

There are many ways the Enneagram can jumpstart your journey and assist you along the way. Although it is a tool that can be used for improving your relationships with others, the truth is that the best relationship to start working on first is the one with yourself. Not to say that you're the only issue in your relationships, but studies show that people with low self-esteem are more likely to remain in existing relationships and attract new ones that are unhealthy or ones in which they're mistreated. Dr. Juliana Breines says that there's ample evidence that negative feelings towards oneself can get in the way of relationships and that people with low self-esteem underestimate the love their partner has for them. They tend to view their partners in a more negative light, and they report that they're less happy with their relationship and feeling negative about its future (Breines, 2016).

One of the great things about the Enneagram is that it shows you what it looks like to be on the healthy, average, and unhealthy sides of your type. This is a unique feature of the Enneagram, and it allows for some real introspection and planning on your part. When we know what it looks like to be healthy, we can more effectively work towards being that way. When we know our tendencies to slip into unhealthy habits, motives, or behaviors in general, we can better prepare for breaking the cycle. We can prioritize, plan, and keep digging and growing along the way.

Empathy is another way the Enneagram can help us improve. Not only is empathy a great skill for us to have in relation to others, but self-compassion is also important. Self-compassion is self-empathy, and the Enneagram can help us figure out how we can use empathy for not only others, but for ourselves as well through typing. Dr. Emma Seppala explains that scientific data shows that self-criticism makes us weaker when we encounter failure. It makes us less likely to learn from our failures; self-compassion is better and healthier for us. She goes on to say that self-compassion may be seen as weakness or self-indulgent, though it is the secret to being resilient, showing strength in failure, and learning from our failures and getting back to it with more energy (Seppala, 2014).

The Enneagram is akin to mindfulness in the sense that you are being aware, honest, and non-judgmental with yourself. Taking a mindfulness approach to the Enneagram will serve anyone well. The core goals in the practice of mindfulness are being focused and present while working on yourself, as well as keeping your self-compassion high and your judgements low. Also remember to be patient with yourself. Some things are easier (and more effectively done) by walking rather than running. You can only know what you know, and pacing yourself on this path will allow you the time and mental space to soak it all in.

Figuring out your next steps is difficult if you do not have a map and have never taken this route before. Bombarding yourself with too much information and trying to do and change too much all at once is more likely to lead to failure. If you pace yourself, working out one step at a time and learning as you grow, you're much more likely to succeed. It can take anywhere from a few weeks to a few months to break a bad habit and replace it with a healthy one. If you try to change your entire life in one go, you're less likely to succeed and keep at it, but if you make smaller changes and really stick to them, they're much easier to accomplish. A part of this may be that you can more easily see and track any changes and soak in more the less you spread yourself out.

Enneagram for Self-Improvement and Introspection

There are many exercises to use the Enneagram on your journey. Much of what you are doing will depend on at what point in your journey you are. There's one piece of advice that's helpful at any point on your path, and that is to always ask yourself why. Digging deeper and finding root causes is an integral part of working through this. It's also very important to listen to and be honest with yourself. Above all, that's the most critical thing you can do on a journey such as this.

You'll find that once you have gotten to know yourself a bit better, you'll be able to distinguish patterns in your life and in your behaviors. These actions and patterns are often unconscious thoughts, thought patterns, and even actions. These patterns set off reactions in your life, driving it at will. Observing what your patters are without judgement will allow you to break the cycle and detach yourself from them and from the things that set them off or aid them along the way.

Studying the Enneagram allows us to see where we differ from others. This is an important step in building healthy, strong, budding relationships with others. Seeing differences not only allows us to appreciate the people around us, but they also help us look at where we shine and in what areas could use some work. The Enneagram gives us the tools for effective conflict resolution should it arise. If you know how to defuse a situation or even avoid it to begin with by typing, that's a big stress out of the lives of everyone involved. Not everyone sees the world in the same way you do, so different people will perceive a situation differently. If four people all witness the same event or situation and you then interview each witness, you'll likely notice that they each noticed something different, slightly different, or something else entirely than what the others did.

The Enneagram provides us all with the same language and knowledge in a lot of senses. There are some excellent uses for this in business and leadership work, as well. Empathy and understanding people's differences is an important practice to work on.

The Enneagram can also help you by reducing stress and providing avenues for coping and dealing with stress. It helps reduce suffering and aids you in coping by preparing you and bringing to light the line of disintegration you follow. In turn, using the Enneagram this way can help you be a more effective, productive, and most importantly, a happier person. As you discover your patterns and learn to break cycles and to be more mindful of how you approach situations and life, you'll find you're able to handle more issues more easily.

With improvement of self, you'll probably notice your relationships naturally improving. You will also find it easier to read people, avoid or resolve conflicts more easily, and be more empathetic towards your family and friends. Another place where you'll observe the

Enneagram can serve you well is in a working position. This is especially true if you're a leader in your work force or if you coordinate any kind of group or team. Knowing types can allow you to steer and run more smoothly. Knowing what people need from you is an excellent way to keep morale up.

As you dive deeper into self, you may find that there are things about you that you didn't even realize, such as hidden desires that you have, new talents, or things you want to be good at. You may find that you need to adjust the path your life is on in an aspect of your life, like your career or hobbies, or you might discover talents you weren't aware of or, if you are being honest with yourself, things you aren't so good at (and that's okay, as we all have things we are good at and things we are not so great at). This can lead you on a more open and honest path, perhaps allowing you to discover a different purpose to your life. You might be surprised by what you find when you keep yourself open and honest going forward.

Try to keep your focus on your motives and intentions instead of your behavior, especially at first. You should start asking yourself why whenever you can, going deeper into a conversation with yourself and your core ("How To Change Your Life Using The Enneagram—Part 2:

Discover Your Type", 2016). When you focus on your intentions and motives, you are focusing on the basis of everything and the purity of the thing you're doing or wanting to do. When it comes down to it, everything we do has a motive or intention behind it, even if it is not one of much note. Our intentions and motives will, if we are honest about them, give us a pretty clear picture of where and who we are as a person. It can be a good way to gage what you need to work on, and it can even help type you in some cases. It's important to check in with yourself often.

Rose and Ben started their Enneagram self-discovery in a funny way but they embraced it and made it work for them. They found that even after 20 years of marriage, there was still a lot to discover about each other. Rose shares their story for us:

I came across the Enneagram kind of by accident. My boss had gotten me to take a personality test at work earlier that week. I was in line for a promotion, and they like to give them to people they are considering. I had never taken one before that day and found myself very interested in the results I was presented with. They made me wonder if I took another kind of personality test if I would get a similar result. I didn't know much about personalities; they seemed very diverse to me, like no two people really had the same one. I suppose in a sense that is kind of true, we are all our own people. Anyway, I searched online and started going through the results. My results ranged from colours to animals and numbers to countries even. There was no shortage of entertainment with the results I was getting. I happened to come across a link for the Enneagram and took the test. My detailed results after that test felt so spot on for me. I even read it to my husband, and he did his. On the results page, he noticed the symbol and was reading the description about what it was with the number type personalities and how they all connect. We went far down the rabbit hole that night. We read about our types and how we take on traits from other numbers depending on our mental health. The fact that it was all so detailed and interesting is what got us hooked. The next day, we found ourselves talking about it again. My husband had been doing a lot of self-help book reading and is always interested in improving himself. He was telling me about how we could use the types to dig into this more. We bought some books and joined a few groups online. We read everything we could get our hands on, and it turned into a fun but important project we were doing together. We were using the techniques we were learning from others and applying them to our *types to make changes in our lives. We had many realizations on our own, but we found that most of all, our relationship was doing so much better. I started to feel like I really understood Ben. I thought I had known him before, and sure, I did in some ways, as we have been married for 20 years, but I was learning things about him I had no clue about. Looking back on our lives now, I can see things I missed before. Times when I was mad at him for being mad or had an issue with him, I can now see why he was acting the way he was, and a lot of the times, it was also my fault, and it was me in distress that was causing him distress. We're much more aware of our inner thoughts and feelings now. We try not to let them affect us, but when they do, we talk it out and make it right. I think being together for so long made learning new things about each other so much more interesting. It's like, how did I not know all of this about you? I mean, you can't get all of it from just reading the descriptions, but you get it from opening up the dialog and looking for the cues in behavior change. We have gone to classes and joined groups, and we have had a lot of fun learning about ourselves and putting it to use for us as a couple.*

5 Exercises for Self-discovery Using the Enneagram

There are many different exercises you can partake in using the Enneagram during your self-discovery journey. It's often helpful for people to have some structured activities when first starting out or even farther into their journey to guide them and push them forward. The following list is not in any particular order.

1. Read through the Enneagram personality types and take the test. Even if you have already done this, rereading the types is helpful. The more you study the Enneagram and the better you know the types, the more you'll be able to get out of the diagram. Find other descriptions by different sources of the types that have things worded differently or perhaps ones that are more detailed than others you've read; this will bring you new insights or may help something fall into place.

2. Meditation is a fantastic tool to utilize during your self-discovery and self-improvement, and it's also ideal for upkeep. You can do this a couple of ways depending on your experience with meditation and your comfort level. You can either meditate on your

own or use guided meditations to facilitate thoughts, change, and growth. Through meditation, you can learn more about yourself and your needs, wants, desires, and fears; really, the list is endless. This is a great way to have an honest discussion with yourself.

3. Get more out of your mind and self through journaling. This doesn't have to be an extensive every day project, although the more you do it, the more you can get out of it. You can write out notes, questions you have, thoughts, wants, where you would like to go, or just a stream of conscious writing - whatever works for you. This exercise can help you keep track of your progress, keep you up to date on what you're doing and where you would like to go, and work out issues you are facing, such as fears. Also, this is an excellent opportunity to have an honest and open conversation with yourself.

4. If you are a religious or spiritual person, the Enneagram can be looked at through a religious or spiritual scope. Using your belief system, you can discover places where you may need to improve and connect them with your beliefs, working

through any discrepancies you may have. This can make your beliefs stronger by causing you to feel more connected by rooting what is important to you as you progress. For example, if you are a Christian, you can find scripture that lends to what you are discovering. There are books available on this specific subject.

5. Ask yourself a question and use your type and answer as well as you can in the way each type would respond. Compare these answers with what your own honest answer would be. This can be an interesting activity for a couple to do, especially while learning the different types.

Chapter 5 : Using the Enneagram in Your Relationship

Love is a common subject for humans all over the world. We strive for it, can't get enough of it, sing about it, write about it, and shout about it from the rooftops. Love is good; love is great, actually. It makes us feel unstoppable, supported, and ready for anything. Two people that choose to be a team and commit to one another is a special thing, an amazing feeling, and something we all like to hold on to. Unfortunately, because we consider love to be so high on our list of needs, it can also be incredibly painful - especially when we lose it.

Ultimately, the Enneagram is a tool to help you reframe your perspective. It helps you see things about yourself and about others and brings you on a journey of self-discovery and self-improvement. When we reframe the way we look at ourselves and others, breaking it down into our motivations and not just actions or simple personality test, we are able to change and improve what happens in our lives. Using the Enneagram to reframe your perspective to improve your relationship is one of its many effective uses.

While the Enneagram is not a substitute for marriage counseling or therapy in more dire situations, it is an effective way to understand yourself and your partner. Doing so improves your relationship and opens up the opportunity for you both to grow together. In order to do all of this, you have to be working on self and you will have to have open and honest conversations with your partner. You'll find yourself reading your partner more than usual and in more depth. Don't be put off if your partner is returning the attention and reading you too; it means they are paying attention just like you, which is a positive thing.

Why Use the Enneagram in Your Relationship?

What does the Enneagram have to offer to your relationship? As already discussed, using the Enneagram for yourself will improve your relationships as a result. It's also hard not to try to type people once you dive into this. When it comes down to it, you will notice things without people telling you now that your eyes are open to it. Although it's difficult to avoid doing, it's best to have your partner type themselves rather than attempting to type them on your own. Perhaps showing them what your type is will interest them enough to take the test and read about the types to figure out their own. Knowing your partner's type will most certainly offer a great advantage for being able to overcome hurdles and anticipate their needs. There are plenty of ways the Enneagram can provide help and value to your relationship, as outlined below.

1. **Compassion and empathy**- Understanding one another is an amazing ability for any relationship. However, this can be hard to do. Using you and your partner's type, you'll be better able to come to a level of compassion and empathy for one another. This will allow for faster and more effective conflict resolution and even the avoidance of conflict altogether. When it comes down to it, one of the most important things in any relationship is respect. Respect and empathy go well together, though they aren't the same thing. You can always respect your partner, even when you do not necessarily understand them or get where they're coming from. It is respect that will help keep your relationship healthy and functioning. Respect will go a long way on its own, but if you add some genuine understanding and empathy along with it, your relationship can truly thrive. The Enneagram is an excellent tool in both cases.

2. Conflict resolution and avoidance- As mentioned above, the Enneagram as a whole can provide great insights into people, which aids in faster and more effective conflict resolution or avoidance. Being able to understand where your partner is coming from, what motivates them, and why something might upset them more than someone else is a unique perspective the Enneagram provides you with (it's up to you to use the knowledge you have gained). This can be as simple as knowing how much conflict upsets a type nine and what you can say or do to ease it for them. For example, if you're dealing with a type nine, instead of upsetting them further with more confrontation, you can change the tone of the conversation, which typically will reduce conflict with this type.

3. **It can make you more humble-** We all have faults and strengths, and the Enneagram helps us identify those in ourselves. It can be hard to see these traits in ourselves otherwise, and many relationships have rocky patches because of this. When you can see where your shortcomings are, you are better able to work on them, make up for them, and embrace them, which can be extremely beneficial for a relationship. It can allow some open and honest conversations to be had which can also create more trust and understanding in a relationship.

Knowing where you may be falling a little short can also help you see where some of your partner's frustrations lie and vice versa. No one is perfect; it is through self-discovery that we learn and come to terms with this and, as a result, we improve.

4. **Highlight your strengths**- Just as everyone has areas they can work on, we also all have areas we excel in. The Enneagram can help you see where your strengths are, just as they can your downfalls. You and your partner should be celebrating and using these strengths to your advantage. Celebrate each other and your wins, have fun, and connect during these positive moments.

5. **Communication**- Communication is key in any relationship. Without it, we're all just living in our own little world and guessing at everything. That sounds exhausting and not like something that anyone wants to really do. There are many benefits to opening up the lines of communication. Everything doesn't have to be positive, but discussing even the most mundane and simple things can bring people closer together. When people can communicate effectively, they're able to thrive and work together. Having open and honest discussions without judgement allows for the sharing of feelings, fears, and desires, not just on the surface, but at the core of each of

us. These kinds of conversations have incredible benefits for any relationship.

Areas of Your Relationship in Which the Enneagram Can Help

There is nothing better than knowing that someone else in this world genuinely understands you. It can be the most exciting experience to find someone who just gets you. These are the types of relationships people strive for and the ones that people think can only appear magically through sheer luck. This is not the case, though. It is something that can be learned and practiced. You have the ability to come to a great understanding for your partner - even if you are complete opposites.

There is no one you want to understand more than your partner, and who does not want that back in return? It's never too late to get a deeper understanding of the person you love. Here are three ways the Enneagram can help you strengthen your understanding:

4. **Core fears-** The Enneagram offers insights into fears that surround a person. Often, many of our traits, motivations, and behaviors are based on the things we fear most. Knowing where your partner's fear comes from will help you understand where

much of their conflict may stem from. When you can understand this, you're better able to support and comfort them, avoid conflict, and deal with conflict in more effective ways. Conflict won't stop, because it is a normal part of the human experience; however, it can be handled and dealt with in a simpler way, and it can certainly happen less. The more someone feels understood and supported, the better they will be able to cope and get back on track to integration and happiness.

5. **Motivation-** The Enneagram offers insight into people's general motivations in life, such as what they do, what they pursue, and why they pursue certain things. Knowing this about your partner is an excellent place to start. Being aware of what drives, inspires, and motivates someone to do things can help you to be more attentive and supportive of that person, and it will allow you to dig deeper. We are not talking about superficial things, here (although in some cases, that may very well be the case), but rather the deeper core desires we all have that are similar to the fears above.

6. **Emotions-** It can be hard for many people to feel vulnerable by sharing their emotions honestly, even

within a loving relationship. The Enneagram can assist in figuring out what is driving any kind of moods or mood changes. It can show us when our partners are doing well and healthy and also when they are not doing so well. Knowing this allows you to put the proper precautions and support into place. Sometimes this is hard to see in ourselves, as we may know it's happening but perhaps not why. When partners can help us be on top of this, they can start pointing it out to us in a helpful way, which is a good spot to begin.

Spiritual Relationships with the Enneagram

The Enneagram has become very popular in certain religious and spiritual circles. There's something to be said for using the Enneagram in such cases - especially as it relates to your own relationships. The Enneagram is a unique tool to develop self-awareness, and that fits well into a spiritual context

Because the Enneagram is rooted in ancient wisdom, it lends itself well to modern day spiritual people. Tools that already exist specifically for spirituality have concepts that are often difficult to grasp or their executions are too abstract.

Depending on your beliefs, the Enneagram can be used to deepen your connection with self, but it can also deepen your connection with a higher power. In this sense, it can be used to map out your spirituality or your religious motivations. Using the Enneagram to do this gives you a clearer picture of yourself and shines a light on your motives or your fears to uncover what drives you. Many beliefs out there strive for and encourage self-improvement and to be the best you can be.

In many households and relationships, spiritual beliefs are something that are fundamental to them. If this sounds like you and your relationship with spirituality, the Enneagram can also be used to strengthen the connection of your relationship to a higher power.

This is something you can do together as a couple, as well. You can introduce your spiritual beliefs however you see fit. There's room for them in this system, and there is much to be learned about yourself through the lens of your beliefs. This is why the two have become a popular pairing and definitely aid each other. If it helps you to use things like scripture to set your goals or provide you with more self-awareness, that's absolutely something that you can do within your own individual Enneagram journey and through the journey of your relationship.

Enneagram 2 manuscripts in 1

Chapter 6 : The Personality Types in Relationships

While it's true that some types may naturally get along better with certain types, that does not mean that all of us cannot thrive together. Although we are looking at types, we have to remember we're also talking about individual people. There are no two types that are better off together than any other two types, but each pairing will have its own unique challenges and strengths. Life circumstances, where an individual falls within their type (healthy, unhealthy, average), and an individual's subtype will also add some complexity to the mix. What makes relationships work and thrive is each partners' willingness to make them work and thrive. Partners need to be able to resolve conflict, know how to support one another, and be willing to work towards being a better and happier couple. Even if you already have a wonderful relationship, we all have room for improvement and growth; those things never cap off.

Types in Relationships

Type One

Type ones are the reformers; they are the perfectionists, and they bring this aspect of themselves into every area of their life. They can make great partners in the sense that they're always trying to improve and do things the correct way. They also have a strong sense of right and wrong, which lends itself to loyalty and dedication. They're wonderful advocates and teachers, which are often good qualities to have in an equal partnership. Type ones will stick up for you and speak up when you cannot.

Because they like to make things go well and turn out right, you might find that a one will try to adjust things about you, as well. A one will typically appreciate it when you take charge and responsibility for these things in a relationship too.

Ones enjoy feeling like they have done well, so acknowledge their efforts and let them know you appreciate all they do and how much they try. A one may need to be reminded to take it easy sometimes, and they appreciate it when their partner helps them balance that out.

Ones can be hard on themselves when something doesn't go as planned - this is in all areas of their life. They may take it particularly hard if they fail or do something "wrong" in a relationship with someone they love, respect, and truly care about. This does not give them an excuse for any behavior that may not be acceptable in a relationship, but they may be too hard on themselves for small things. This is best to keep an eye out for; it's possible they'll need reassurance after a confrontation with a loved one.

When they're at their best, ones can be very faithful, dedicated, fun, attentive, and helpful. When they are at their worst, they can be stubborn, pick fights, expect absolute perfection from everyone, and be very critical.

Type Two

Type twos (the helpers) are the people pleasers. Twos can be great partners, because they're very attentive to others' needs and wants. They want their partner to have a great experience, and they're friendly, generous, and empathic people, making them easy to have an open and honest conversation with. They like the connection this can provide, and they strive for that in their relationships.

Twos care very much about how their partner perceives them and what they think about them. They want to do well in their relationships, and they can take it hard when they don't. Their emotions can take over during times of conflict, as they're an emotional group and can be fairly sensitive, which is something to be cautious of.

Twos make great supportive partners; their traits make it easier to deal with difficult and delicate situations that require empathy and compassion. They will do whatever they can to make things go well for you, even at their own expense. They have a tendency to live through their partners for this reason. They are nurturing and like to play this role.

Twos need to be told to take care of themselves, as well; this can be hard for them to accept, but they'll appreciate you ensuring they are cared for. Being a people pleaser can be an exhausting role.

When they're at their best, twos can be very nurturing, attentive, caring, generous, and experts at making you feel loved. When they're at their worst, they can be too needy, clingy, insecure, insincere, and controlling.

Type Three

Type threes are the achievers. They're driven people who are drawn to success. When a three wants something, they go for it, and they do not like to fail. Threes tend to be workaholics, but the good news is that they can put that kind of energy into their relationships, as well.

Threes like to know they're appreciated and respected for how hard they work. They also need someone to remind them to balance out their life. A three needs encouragement and to know that they're doing well. When they feel like they can succeed in something, they will go all in. Praise is great for threes, but they can get defensive, so be cautious in your criticism. They can handle it if done gently and in a way where they can easily see a means for improvement.

Threes need their partners to help them balance out their life, and they appreciate the work and attention their partner puts into them, since they work very hard themselves. Threes also have a tendency to like to work alone and need space. This is not something their partner should take personally; this is simply how they are. When you encourage something outside of their work, do so in a gentle way, as they can take it the wrong way.

When they're at their best, threes can be energetic, responsible, generous, and hard working, yet able to balance. When they're at their worst, they can be too self-absorbed, impatient, defensive, unforgiving, dishonest, and far too preoccupied with work.

Type Four

Type fours (the individualists) are highly creative and sensitive people. They like to surround themselves with beauty and are often very skilled in the creative fields. You should expect this to flow into their relationships. Fours make fun partners because of these traits. They're the romantic type, and they know how to use this to their advantage. Fours are the people that will use you as a muse for their paintings, music, or writing, and it is certainly a high compliment from a four if they do so. However, they do enjoy getting some romance in return.

Fours are not afraid to show you their emotions or tell you what they are thinking, as they often wear their heart on their sleeves, which keeps their partner from guessing. This is a particularly good quality to have in a relationship, though fours can get too emotional and be overly sensitive. They're more often susceptible to negative moods and attitudes because of their heightened sensitivity. They often need help and appreciate someone who helps them get through a low time. Fours also appreciate honest compliments that help bring their spirits up, and, when at their best, they're good at doing the same.

Fours can be energetic, fun, creative, generous, and empathetic. When they're at their worst, they can be angry, depressed, moody, and too clingy or emotionally needy.

Type Five

Type fives are the investigators, and they're intense people. They bring this intensity into their relationships in both positive and negative ways. They're also perceptive people, which is a great quality in a partner.

Fives tend to like to be alone, and they're often very introverted people. They enjoy spending time with their partner in quieter settings where they can really talk and explore concepts together. If you find yourself partnered with a five, it's best not to take their need to be alone personally; it's not anything against you. Fives can make very interesting conversationalists. They have great knowledge about many things, but are usually particularly knowledgeable about one specific topic. They like to be able to share their thoughts and what they know with others. Fives love to learn, and when they are interested in something, they will work on knowing everything they can about it. Don't be surprised if a type five asks you a lot of questions when they're interested in you.

Fives can feel insecure and distance themselves. When this happens, they appreciate a partner that knows when to give them the space they need and when to reassure them. When they're at their best, fives can be perceptive, kind, great teachers, creative, and open. When they're at their worst, they can be suspicious, withdrawn, and cold.

Type Six

The type six is the loyalist. These are a committed and hardworking people. They're loyal in their relationships as they are in much of their lives. They like to feel secure and give that back in return. Sixes need to feel supported, and they thrive with a partner who is able to provide this for them.

Sixes tend to take on a lot of responsibility, often shouldering it for their partner. They're also great problem solvers, which makes them especially good at conflict resolution; both are positive qualities to have in a partner. Where sixes need a little help and tend to falter is when they take on too much and have too much stress in their lives. This stress can weigh them down when it's too high, but it's also a balancing act for them; they have the ability to thrive in high stress situations. Sixes appreciate a partner that can point out to them when they need to allow themselves to regain balance to stay well. Too much stress can make a six high strung, snappy, defensive, and anxious. When sixes show their fun side, it's best for their partner to encourage and celebrate it. After all that hard work and stress, they need to let loose.

When they're at their best, sixes can be committed, loyal, hardworking, fun, honest, and supportive. When at their worst, they can be too needy, insecure, controlling, and anxious.

Type Seven

Type sevens (the enthusiasts) are very high energy people. They are especially fun to be around and make for a great time. If your partner is a seven, you are sure to have a lot of fun adventures and experiences.

Their bubbly positive attitude can be infectious, and they're often the life of the party wherever they go. While not a particularly committed group of people, they are practical. Sevens appreciate a partner that can go with the flow and look at the bigger picture. They appreciate someone who keeps them a little more grounded, but they do thrive on variety and need it in their lives.

When a seven finds something or someone they're interested in, they're immediately enthralled and enthusiastic about it. Sevens like their partners to be around and are certainly one of the most extroverted people you will come across. They do not appreciate trying to be changed but may appreciate some gentle nudges to slow down when they need to. Sevens appreciate someone who will have fun with them and get caught up in their affairs just as much as they do.

When they're at their best, sevens can be adventurous, fun, enthusiastic, generous, and quick thinkers. When they're at their worst, they can be self-centered, distracted or scatterbrained, and irresponsible.

Type Eight

Type eights are the challengers. They're dominant and assertive people. This can make them misunderstood by others and cause some challenges in their relationships. Eights often do not mean to be intimidating (especially to their partners), but they can easily come across this way. If you find yourself facing this issue with your type eight partner, it's best to be honest with them about it.

When eights let their vulnerable side show, it's a good idea to be gentle with them and let them know that it's okay. Eights may have a tough exterior, but they have soft spots like anyone else. Eights appreciate someone who will stand up to them; they aren't afraid of confrontation and often don't shy away from it. While you do not need to be picking fights with anyone, if you find that there's a reason to say something to an eight partner, it's best to do it directly and assertively. They appreciate that sense of directness that often makes them intimidating to other people.

Eights tend to be self-confident people. They don't need their partners to overly compliment them, but they do appreciate the reminder. Eights will also value the acknowledgement of their softer and more loving side when they show it. Let them know you like and appreciate that in them, and that gentle nudge will help to encourage them to show it more often. Because eights like to be in control, this can sometimes be exactly what they need reminding of in a relationship - that they are equal to their partner.

When they're at their best, eights can be honest, caring, loyal, courageous, supportive, and loving. When at their worst, they can be too aggressive, demanding, self-centered, stubborn, and argumentative.

Type Nine

Type nines (the peacemakers) are all about maintaining peaceful interactions and balance in their lives and relationships. Nines are loyal and committed people in relationships who are not argumentative and prefer things to run as smoothly as possible. This is sometimes to a fault, and they will go with the flow a little too much to ensure this happens, sometimes pushing themselves aside to keep the peace.

Nines hate conflict; it's something they avoid whenever they can. If you have a nine partner, one of the ways you can show them how much you care is to avoid confronting them with conflict and to respect their disdain for it. This is not to say you can't bring up an issue you may be having, but rather that you do it in a way that is not confrontational. Nines will appreciate an open conversation, even if it makes them uncomfortable. It's an argument that will make them feel unwelcome in a fundamental way.

Nines may seem as though they don't care about an issue you're having. They can downplay negative situations and feelings because it's something that they don't handle well. Know that this is not personal to you or anyone else; they often care but do not want to be in the middle of the negativity.

Nines make great partners, and they're trusting, honest, and positive. They are embracing and accepting to people in general, but this is amplified for their partners. They can be very understanding and make a good support system. They're known to go with the flow and accept things at face value without judgement. Nines are committed people that thrive on stability, and this makes them wonderful long-term partners.

Nines prefer to be around someone who appreciates their need for positive balance. They're often creative people and like to have fun. They like to be around people and fear being separated from them. This is an important realization for someone in a partnership with a nine, since much of their insecurities can stem from this.

When they are at their best, nines can be honest, caring, loyal, non-judgemental, gentle, peaceful, and supportive. When at their worst, they can be too accommodating, stubborn, defensive, and withdrawn when threatened with conflict.

Chapter 7 : 7 Key Areas that Control Your Partner's Behavior

Emotions, core traits, beliefs, needs, and desires are what drive people to do most things they choose to do. An individual's behavior is often based on deeper inner workings. There are seven areas in which we can focus our understanding of the core areas that motivate your partner's behavior; these include anger, fear, distress, joy, desire, purpose, and needs. Much of these things are not usually created through conscious thought, but are the subtle underlying force that makes you work the way you do. Have you ever wondered why some people will more readily jump into an argument with their partner every chance they get or why your partner may be suddenly distant? Many times, it doesn't have much to do with you, but rather what is going on for them.

Perception is everything to people. How one sees something may be sees a totally different way by another person. The best way to know is to ask, but let's go over some of the options. Sometimes we are not sure why we do what we do or why we act how we act; our inner workings are not always conscious thoughts or things that we're acknowledging.

Anger- Anger is an emotion that drives us in some of the most intense ways possible. Depending on the situation and how we handle this emotion, it can be anything from a flash of all encompassing, blackout anger or an annoyance that seethes within when holding a grudge. Anger is an emotion that can stem from others, with fear being one of the most likely causes. It is our way of protecting ourselves; lashing out and pushing others away is a protective mechanism we've developed. The Enneagram can help distinguish types that are more prone to anger or how they handle it. For example, you may find a type eight to be someone who tends to get angry and does not hide their emotions. Is there an eight in your life that is spending more time at the gym and letting their anger out in moody bursts? The need for a physical release of anger is telling. Their quick snips of anger towards you may be them trying to avoid being angry with you, but it is slipping out anyway.

Fear- Fear is at the base of what paths we decide to take, our feelings, and our behavior. Fear guides us in both positive and negative ways. It's a feeling that exists to protect us from harm. While physical harm is a danger for everyone, the things that can harm us mentally, emotionally, and through our ego can range widely from person to person and from type to type. You'll find that fear can be the base for other emotions, such as distress, anger, and increased anxiety. Fear is also telling of what we need, want, what makes us happy, and what we desire. It's often the threat of loss of those things that causes what we fear, and our reaction to it is the behavior set by other protective emotions such as anger. For example, type fives fear being useless or helpless. Because of this, they pride themselves in being knowledgeable and self-reliant. If your type five partner is feeling fear, you may find them being more scatterbrained and active on their line of disintegration into an unhealthy seven. Their being more active and scatterbrained may be an example of their anxious energy in the face of fear.

Distress- Distress is any kind of negative stress you may find in your life. This can be be the result of things like an upsetting event or even something along the lines of stress being piled on from work. Stress can cause us to fall into disintegration, especially when we're having trouble coping. If you find that your loved one is not doing well, you may not be able to put your finger on why, but their mood and actions will often be a good indicator of this. Even if just subtly, it is best to check in with them. You may find that distress can lead to a very wide range of behaviors depending on one's type and the situation. The level of stress and how well your partner is doing will determine what behaviors may be occuring.

Joy- Joy can bring on many behaviors in us, as well, with many of them being positive. It's with joy that we often find ourselves along the line of integration. You may find your partner thriving, happier, and more affectionate in these situations. Joy drives us to continue to pursue things that bring us joy; this feeling is addictive to us, and rightly so. Encourage your partner when they're here, and celebrate with them. Their behavior may not cause any concern in this place, but this emotion will drive their behavior, usually to more healthy and positive things for them and for you as well.

Desire- Desire can be described as being the feeling we have when we want something very profoundly that it has a great impact on our thoughts and behaviors, with both conscious and subconscious thought processes going on. We are often very aware of what we desire or yearn for, especially when it's strong and in the forefront. We have base desires, as well, though sometimes we're not as aware of them. When they're not being fulfilled, you can have negative behaviors happen, even leading into disintegration. When they're being met or acknowledged, they can lead to more positive behaviors and ones that encourage more growth. Fundamentally, our base desires are what we want in life. If you find your partner is suddenly more distracted, it may be because they're working towards something to help fulfill this. For example, one of type nine's driving desires is for peace and balance in their lives. If they're being bombarded by stress and conflict, that can send them down to disintegration, affecting their behavior either way they go.

Purpose- Everyone needs a purpose to fulfill in life. This can be something that makes up who you are at your core and your fundamental purpose in life, or it can be something that's found more on the surface. It's healthy for us as humans to feel as though we are serving a purpose, as humans thrive on and live for a purpose to guide them. When we're feeling as though we do not have purpose or that we are not fulfilling it to our own standards, our feelings, thoughts, and behaviors can shift into something more negative. This can lead someone on a path of disintegration.

Needs- Needs are another core thing we have that can bring on either positive or negative thoughts or behavior. The term "needs" is very broad; it can mean anything. For these purposes, we are talking about core needs - things people need to continue living. What your needs are will depend on you as a person, your health, and your Enneagram type. It is here where you will find a similar answer to needs as purpose. A person who is fulfilling their needs or working towards them may seem happier, be more affectionate, and possibly be more distracted with more on their plate than usual. Behaviors will lead towards integration personally, as well as within a relationship, if needs are not being met.

Real Life Key Areas

Damien and Patricia have been together for ten years. Their relationship could be much better - that they both admit. Damien happens to be an eight and Patricia a nine. On recalling their relationship before they began their Enneagram journey, Patricia often felt as though she was being too controlled and was always faced with confrontation. She felt like she was giving too much of herself. She recounts their journey over the last couple of years and their experience with the Enneagram:

Looking back over the last ten years, I realized how out of control I felt, and how uneven our relationship felt. I wasn't able to push back on things I wanted and often felt stressed out. I didn't know how to express to Damien that I was feeling this way. Whenever I tried, it led to a fight, so I would let it go. But I wouldn't really let it go, you know? It was always there in the back of my mind. I love this man so dearly, and I am so happy to be with him, and I want to be with him. But I was feeling done after so many years of this. I don't want to make him sound bad, because he's not bad. He doesn't constantly fight with me or anything, but I just wasn't able to speak up for myself. He is a loving and supportive man, but he can be very intense, and once we started using the Enneagram for our relationship, I realized that he wasn't even aware of it. He had no idea that I felt the way I did, that I was letting go of things I didn't want to let go of, and that I was making myself unhappy by doing this. When we first started using the Enneagram, we were fighting more than we ever had. We were both so stressed out. I was snapping, because I was frustrated and unhappy, because I didn't know how to tell him what I needed. That was making him snappier and more stressed out, which brought more conflict into my life. I wasn't exactly sure what I needed. When I found the Enneagram and suggest we type ourselves, it opened up so much for us. At first we just shared what our types were and that's when it clicked for me why I had been having so much trouble. It gave me the words I was missing to explain to him what I had been feeling. When we had a sit-down talk about it, I got him to read my type again and then explained what

I had been trying to explain for so long. It was then that he started to understand. In contrast, our types look like they couldn't ever possibly get along. It has been a couple of years now, and we are doing great - better than ever. It wasn't always easy, but we made it work. We have even made our sit-down talks a regular, at least weekly, thing for us. By communicating more often and being more open to that kind of discussion, it really did it for us. We actually had fun learning about the Enneagram together and figuring out ways we could use it for us. We still use it, although now it has just become blended into our everyday. We don't even notice that we do it anymore. It seems that our problem was understanding each other. He had no clue how I was feeling, so he didn't know or understand that I needed him to adjust with me. It took a little bit of time, but he was much more cautious about how he approached me after that. We still butt heads every now and then, like any couple, and I still don't like it, but I handle it better now. We are able to take a step back and work things out. I definitely recommend trying the Enneagram out with your partner if you feel like there is a lack of understanding between you two.

Patricia's take on her relationship with Damien is an interesting but not uncommon one. It's true that on paper, eights and nines do not look like they would get along enough to be in the same room together, let alone live together for an extended period of time. However, any type can get along with any other type. There are no hard and fast be-all-end-all rules to who can be friends and who cannot. Rules like that just do not exist, because they don't work. It's the understanding between people along with respect that enables us all to get along. Patricia made an excellent point about a problem that many couples face; they just do not take the time to talk about what is going on for them. As Patricia also points out, sometimes you don't have the words to describe what's bothering you. She let her distress make her snappy, and that, in turn, made Damien more distressed, which is understandable. For this couple, the Enneagram worked well to mend this, as it does for many. It sounds as though Patricia was feeling like she might need to leave the relationship at that point, though it was obviously something that could be repaired, and it indeed did get worked out in the end. Having an open and honest discussion is the best place to start with any situation.

Take a moment to consider your current or a past relationship. Looking back, do you see points where your actions were driven by feelings or fears, and you didn't talk about or work through these feelings? Knowing what you know now, do you think it's something you could have been more honest with yourself about? The goal is not to ignore your emotions or stress, as everyone has bad things happen and experiences negative emotions; the goal is to be more aware of them and how they affect you and how they may play a role in your partner's behavior.

Chapter 8 : 7 Tips for Bringing the Best Out in Each Other

As partners in a committed relationship, it's important for you both to work on yourselves. However, it's also important to try to bring the best out in one another. Now that you have a good understanding of the Enneagram and the personality types that it encompasses, let's dive into the many ways you can use the Enneagram to bring out the best in both of you.

Imagine what it would be like for both you and your partner to be at your very best, not only individually, but also in your relationship. Using the "Types in Relationships" section, you should be able to get a good feel for what your partner needs and appreciates in a relationship and also what to anticipate when things are not going exactly as planned. Remember that people do not change from their base type, so changing your partner fundamentally is not going to happen; however, each type has its unhealthy, average, and ideal bases that they can move around as the situations arise.

Below are 7 tips to help you navigate with your partner on your journeys of self-discovery together as a couple. Partners can help one another up the line of integration to their best, healthiest, and happiest self. We all want what's best for our loved ones, and what better way to show your love?

7 Tips

1. **Be clear and direct-** Communication is always going to be key in a relationship, but the quality of the communication is what really ups the ante. If you have ever been to another country where they don't speak a language that you do, you'll easily comprehend this tip. When you're not clear and direct with your partner, it can feel like you're speaking another language. Another analogy that may help is talking to someone with a very thick accent that you aren't accustomed to. They may speak the language you do, but what they're saying may be broken, jumbled, or you just may not be able to decipher the message they're trying to convey. Attempting to effectively communicate like this all the time is impossible; someone is going to miss something or misunderstand something. You are often left guessing at what was meant, and you're not a mind reader, so how can you possibly know? When you are clear and direct, you're able to get to the root of things more easily and effectively.

Looking at the Enneagram, you'll find that every type will appreciate this approach. The clearer you are, the more effectively you're able to grow and learn from one another.

2. **Set goals together-** Working towards a goal together is a way to be clear about what you both want and about what the future holds for you. When you know what you want and you can communicate that with your partner, not only will your relationship thrive, but you will also both thrive as individuals. Setting a goal with your partner is akin to working towards your line of integration. It is a plan to get there and get there together. Fostering teamwork with a shared common goal will benefit both of you and bring you closer together. Couples therapist Elliott E. Connie uses the following as an analogy: Imagine getting into a cab, and when the driver asks you where you'd like to go, you say, "Not here." If you don't like where you are, the most logical solution is to figure out where you'd like to be and figuring out how to get there (Tartakovsky, 2018).

3. **Always be learning**- Whether you have been together for five weeks or 35 years, there is always

something to be learned about one another. As beings with depth, inner workings, a past, a present, and desires for the future, there is always more to be learned. Every day that goes by brings us new challenges that help us grow. It's true that our base type does not change, but we do often change around it. Also, there is more to us than a personality type, no matter how accurate it may be. Couples have aspects to learn about their relationship, as well, while looking back, looking at the present, and going forward. Not only will learning improve your growth and strengthen your own self and your relationship, it will also encourage a deeper connection with your partner. Be sure to pay attention to them, set aside time for them specifically, give them a hand, ask questions, and ponder your future together. You should always try to foster your love and help it grow.

4. **Remind them-** One of the best ways you can grow your connection with your partner and help them to be their best is to tell them why it is you love them. Remind your partner that you love them, about what their strengths are, how proud you are of something they have achieved, and what's positive about them. Even people and types that do

not like being overly flattered like a gentle reminder that they're loved, respected, and doing well. Showing your partner that you're not only paying attention, but also that you see so much good and potential in them, is an excellent way to boost their ego and help them to up their game to be the best they can be. When you expect reasonably more from your partner, they'll often meet your expectations. Letting your partner know that you see a lot of untapped potential in them is a great booster for them. Remember to cheer them on as they go. Often, most types will return the enthusiasm and give you a boost, as well. Some types may get a little too caught up in themselves to realize that they can be doing this at all, let alone should, so letting them know you'd like some encouragement as well is not a bad idea. Remember to always be clear and direct.

5. **No one is right, and no one is wrong-** Ditch the "I am right, you are wrong" attitude. Perception is everything, and there are always at least two valid sides to every story. Anita Chlipala, a relationships coach and therapist, says that both people are right. Couples often see people taking turns with who is right and who is wrong, but that

is viewing things with a limited black and white view. "Everyone has a subjective reality that is valid," she explains. She also says that when you disagree with your partner, it does not make your partner wrong; they simply have a different perspective from you. Chlipala continues to say that respecting and validating your partner's feelings and thoughts by trying to understand them and show that the feeling is respected is absolutely necessary for a healthy relationship (Deitz, 2016).

6. **Give space-** Everyone needs their space every now and then to get their thoughts in order, recharge, or do something they enjoy. Allowing your partner to have a life outside of your relationship and home will give them the opportunity to grow, learn, and seek out more potential. It might seem a little counterintuitive, but the time does not have to be long. Always being together is not a bad thing in theory, but in practice, it makes for a tougher time to find things to talk about, and being too needy or clingy are bad things in a relationship. People need room to breathe and add to their experiences. Yes, they can do this with you, but we need to grow as individuals and come back together as a couple to talk about those experiences and the things we

learned. Since it's healthy for people to have hobbies and activities of their own, encourage your partner to explore and learn while you do the same.

7. **Be persistent, be consistent, and check in-** It's important to check in with your partner every now and then. Sit down and discuss what's going on in your lives and what you're excelling in and struggling with. Anything you may be worried or prideful about is important to discuss with your significant other. Discover in what areas you can support them, and be sure you are supported and have back up from the person you love. Checking in at least once a day is a great idea, but if you want to take it up a notch, you could have more than one quick check-in session to ask how their day was. Do this consistently, and it will be easy to notice the improvements. Not only will your partner feel cared for, but they will also open up to you more, and this is an excellent way to facilitate change and growth and to explore more potential.

Bringing out the best in each other doesn't have to be a big, complicated task, but rather can be smaller ones that add up. Much of how our partners feel in this regard is how their partners talk to them. So, adjusting smaller things as you go will add up exponentially as you progress.

Real Life Potential

Shawn, who is a type two, talks about some of the struggles he had with his wife, Amy, who is a four. Shawn and Amy have been married for three years and found themselves in some dark places. After a suggestion from a friend, Shawn decided to try and help Amy see what he sees in her. They implemented a rule where they give each other a compliment each day; they both must say something positive to the other person every single day. Shawn recounts his experience with the challenge that they decided to take on:

I love my wife, but we struggled for a long time. She has had a lot of trouble with her mental health, and that hasn't helped anything for either of us. Our lives were looking pretty dull and bleak. We needed to do something about it; we both needed changes. As a couple and as our own people, we weren't growing. I felt stuck and knew that there had to be something I could do to help us both out. I knew that my wife had so much more to give, but I could see that she wasn't perceiving that in herself. When we got her health sorted out, I wanted to help build her back up. She deserves every ounce of support and every compliment she is given. She's a hard worker and does so much for everyone around her. She wasn't seeing her own potential, though, and I wanted her to, I wanted her to see what I see in her. As we both worked on ourselves individually, it was mentioned to me that I should try to help her out too. I wondered how I could help someone better themselves. I thought that to be something you have to do on your own. My friend told me that he and his wife had been doing this exercise where they give each other a compliment or say something nice and encouraging every day. Each day, they make it a point to shine a light on something good about the other person. I thought that sounded like a great idea. Mark said it had really improved how he thought about his wife. He said that at first, he wasn't so sure about the idea, but he tried it anyway for her. It wasn't that he didn't love his wife and want to tell her that, but I guess he thought it was a little silly, because he thought she would've known that already. I thought my wife knew that I felt this way about her too - that I see so much potential and good in her. I knew she was having trouble seeing it in herself, but I didn't imagine she didn't know that I feel this way. I thought I must tell her enough. After Mark had told me to give it a shot, I brought the idea up to my wife. She agreed to do it with me, though she was probably as skeptical about my odd suggestion as I was when Mark had told me about it. By making myself tell Amy something nice everyday, I quickly realized how little I had actually been doing it before. I mean, I told her I loved her all the time, like when I was leaving for work or before hanging up the phone, but it was more of a reflex to do it - automatic. I thought it was enough, because I was saying it. We both felt similarly, and it felt awkward to compliment each other like this at first, as it was a little obvious that we were forcing it. We kept it up, though, and every day it got a little easier. The more we worked on ourselves and the more we encouraged each other, the more there was to say. I looked forward to my compliment everyday, and so did Amy. We still do this, now, just over a year later. It's something we both look forward to. When we look back at those early days of doing it, it's clear we weren't taking the proper time or putting forth enough energy to really support each other and to really tell each other that we care. We expected that the other person just knew. How could you not just know? Turns out we both didn't. We still have good and bad days, and that will never change, but our days are happier, and the bad days aren't as bad as they once were. I think now, even on bad days or when something stressful is going, on we have a solid base knowing how much we are loved and all the good we see in each other. We have both grown a lot in the past year. I can't speak for Amy, but knowing she believed in me and was behind me made so much of a difference in every part of my own life. Our relationship has improved more than I thought it would. There was so much room for improvement that I didn't notice was actually there. Our compliments turned into real talk, we share everything now, and we aren't afraid to ask if the other person needs something; I think that has been one of the biggest changes for us. And now, when I tell Amy I love her, I try to do it purposefully and not just as a reflex, because I do love her, and she should know that. I don't ever want her to not know that again.

Shawn made some excellent points about himself and his wife. We often say things like "I love you" without giving it a second thought. We can do this much so that it doesn't always register that we have said it or that it was said to us. Shawn and Amy came to find that they needed more than to simply say they love each other before hanging up the phone. Shawn states that he didn't realize how much he needed to hear these things from his wife, as well, and he was shocked when she told him that she didn't know how he really felt about her. This is an important point to show, as people are not mind readers. Unless something is told to us clearly and directly, we can only guess. Often, our perceptions are not the truth, but are instead educated guesses based on the actions of others that we notice. If you aren't telling someone that you love them or about how you feel about them, then how are they really going to know?

This challenge looks like it opened up some great lines of communication for them and did so in a fun and loving way. Shawn and Amy clearly love each other, and as they began to reinforce this, they could see the positive changes in all aspects of their lives. That, in turn, continued to strengthen their relationship and the work they had been doing on it.

Compliment-a-Day Exercise

Give the compliment-a-day exercise a go for yourself. You can use the Enneagram and type descriptions to see some examples of ways your partner may like to be supported or things they may appreciate hearing. You can also see if your partner's type does not necessarily respond well to flattery. If that's the case, you can still do this challenge, but keep this in mind when you're complimenting them. Keep the compliment or nice comment simple in these cases. Obviously, this is something you have to get your partner in on as well, so you will have to get their permission to have them participate. Keep in mind that it's a good idea to track your progress with this challenge, and it can also make it more interesting.

Note how you are feeling when you first start this exercise by asking yourself the following questions:

- Are you finding it easy or difficult to do?
- Are there any immediate changes in mood or otherwise?
- Do you find that you already know your partner feels this way about you?
- How is your partner responding to the challenge?
- What are your first impressions about it?
- How does your impression change over time?
- As some time has passed, do you find it easier or harder to do?
- Are you finding that it helps you?
- What impact has it had on you and on your relationship?

Chapter 9 : Improving Communication in Your Relationship

Through this book, communication has been discussed many times. It's important that two people in a relationship are transparent and communicate as effectively as possible. It's through communication that we're able to make connections with people and keep these connections going. Communication fosters understanding and empathy when done effectively. Like any skill, it requires practice and can take a lot of it before you get it just right. We're always a work in progress with everything we do, and our effective communication skills are no exception to that. Without talking to your partner, you cannot learn enough about them to be able to understand and empathize with them. While the Enneagram is a great tool to get you started with this and can provide some much-needed insight to both parties, it's by talking to your partner that you're able to really dig in deep. It's through discussions with self that you are able to work through your own distress, overcome your fears, and discover yourself.

Studies from the University of Georgia have shown that it's not necessarily communication itself that strengthens a relationship, but instead, the better a couple is able to communicate, the more satisfaction they will experience (Beeson, 2016). More effective communication is absolutely a symptom of a healthier and happier couple, but it's still a skill that needs to be practiced as you go. Setting you and your partner up for positive and effective communication can improve and strengthen a relationship.

Another study published in the Journal of Family Psychology supports this by stating that the way we engage with our partners affects our well-being (LaBier, 2016). Therefore, effective and positive communication and satisfaction in a relationship is interestingly a cycle. Looking at the Enneagram, the connection between people and communication certainly exists. If we think of communication as a cycle and use the Enneagram as a way to improve satisfaction, we can successfully improve both our relationships and our communication, which will in turn continue to improve both of those aspects as we keep going.

Quality time and opportunities to partake in positive communication with your partner will assist you in not only strengthening your relationship, but in allowing you to learn more about one another and to get a better understanding of each other. Below are activities and suggestions for you and your partner to use in order to aid you in your discovery and effective communication as a couple.

16 Activities to Foster Satisfaction and Effective Communication

1. **Active listening-** This is an effective tool to help you practice listening and really hearing what other people are saying. You and your partner can do this together by having one person be the speaker and the other be the listener. The listener's job is to hear what the speaker is saying, and once they are done, repeating what they heard. The goal is not to repeat back what the speaker has said word for word, but rather to tell the speaker what you heard as the listener. The speaker will let you know if you got something wrong or if you missed some information. The point of this activity is to try to actually listen to what someone is saying rather than just hearing it. We can talk all we want, but being able to listen to what someone else is saying is a lot harder for many of us than it sounds. When we aren't listening effectively, we may not be fully understanding what the other person is saying. You can

certainly have fun with this active listening exercise, but it's also a useful skill to have and an important part of effective communication.

2. **Ask questions**- What better way is there to get to know someone more or to understand where they are coming from than by asking questions? But it can't be that simple, can it? Yes, it actually can be. You do not need to interrogate them, but throwing out a question here and there is a good way to strike up a conversation and practice those skills. Also, a good way to get to know someone or to get them talking is to share stories about your past. You can ask your partner what they were like or about their favorite memory as a kid, or perhaps you could ask them things like what their favorite subjects were in school or what they wanted to be when they got older. It's interesting to see what our loved ones wanted and where they ended up. It can reveal a lot about them.

3. **Compliment them**- As we discussed earlier in the book, complimenting your partner is an effective way to build up your relationship. Take some time to compliment them on something you never have before. This could be something they have recently improved on, or maybe even something they did that made you feel good. Let them

know you noticed, and keep building the foundations for a great relationship.

4. **Pray together**- If you are a spiritual couple, one thing you can do together is pray. This is an opportunity to talk to them about what's going on in your life. You can find something you both would like to pray about and do so together. If you're comfortable with talking about what you normally pray about, this can be an effective way to learn new things about your partner. If they're not comfortable answering, that is okay, as this is for them to decide. If you're not a religious person or don't pray, you can do something similar by checking in with your partner to see what's going on; you can even ask them a question along the lines of, "If you could change anything right now, what would it be?"

5. **Meal time**- Slap on those aprons and get cooking together. Preparing a meal with one another is a great opportunity for some fun and communication. You can make a simple meal you both like or make what you can with what you have on hand, creating a dish that's new. This is a good teamwork activity, but it's also fostering fun, satisfaction, and effective communication.

6. **Around the world**- If you could go anywhere in the world, where would it be, and where would your partner

prefer to travel? Discuss your perfect vacation, including everything you'd want to do and see. Do not leave out any details; if you have thought about it, tell them. You can even go ahead and start planning it out on paper. It may not be currently in reach, but it makes a goal and dream for you both to work towards and look forward to. It's also a great opportunity to learn more about your partner and hone those communication skills.

7. **Take on some of your partner's chores**- Taking on some of the things your partner always does allows you to not only give them a bit of a break, but give yourself a chance to see things from their perspective. This doesn't have to be a permanent takeover of your partner's normal responsibilities. You can take on a few things, let them know that you appreciate all that they do, and get a better feel for the things they do. This can be a helpful exercise in understanding your significant other, especially if dissatisfaction or confrontation with them stems from such subjects.

8. **They make you better**- If you feel as though your partner makes you a better person or encourages you in some way, let them know. Have a little talk about how it makes you feel, that you appreciate that they do so, and that you are better for it. When couples can lift each other

up, they're able to accomplish anything they want. Showing your appreciation is a perfect way to foster satisfaction in your relationship.

9. **Memory exercise**- Think back to a good experience you both shared. This could be something like a trip that you went on together or anything that is a shared experience. Talk about it with each other, and remember the good times, but also get into the details of it. Remember the tastes, smells, feelings, what you were thinking, and funny moments you shared. This memory can recreate a good feeling from a happy time in your relationship. It can also create conversation, not only about that memory, but about plans you can make to create more memories in the near future.

10. **Ask them to be your umbrella**- This is a funny way to say ask your partner to let you poor out something in order to protect yourself. If you have something that's making you anxious or particularly distressed, ask your partner if you can use them to let it out. They do not have to say or do anything aside from listen. You can empty out what is making you stressed out, explain it away, and let the negative emotion leave you. You may think this sounds counterintuitive, since you want to create satisfaction rather than venting everything to them and

making them stressed. However, you need to be able to confide in your partner and discuss negative things with them. The point of this is not to stress them out, as they don't need to offer a way to fix anything; they just need to listen so you can get it all off your chest. This is an activity that will make the person letting it out feel better and allow the person listening to gain a deeper understanding of their partner and where they may be heading now. Both partners can do this for each other.

11. **Apologize**- There is a lot of power in an apology - especially a genuine one. Think back to something you may have done to your partner that you should have apologized for but never did. Apologize to them for it now so you can clear the air. We cannot be right all of the time, no matter how much we insist we are. Being able to apologize is a healthy step when we aren't right. This enables healthier and more transparent conversations.

12. **Go on a spontaneous adventure**- Go out and have fun together! Create great memories that will allow for some wonderful conversations later. After all, everyone needs some fun in their lives. Couples absolutely benefit from spending quality time together. Something like this adds some spice to your life and can make for some

opportunities you would not have thought of or done otherwise.

13. **I'm angry**- The next time your partner does something that upsets or distresses you, take a moment to figure out why it's affecting you in such a way. Were they purposely trying to get under your skin or are you reacting to other things going on in your mind or life at the moment? Don't let the negative emotions stew; let your partner know that you're upset and explain to them why, even if it's not actually what they're doing that is making you upset. It's important to let them know the real reason why you are in distress and that whatever they did triggered that for you. At the very least, it gives them some insight into what's happening in your life and also in your mind at that moment. It allows them the space to support you and be understanding.

14. **Read**- Create your own little book club with just the two of you. Read the same book, and discuss it when you're done. It is best to set a timeline on how long you have to read it. Also be sure to avoid giving away any spoilers during reading. Having a common activity, especially one that you can keep on doing, is a great way to inspire closeness. Something like a book club also brings effective and interesting conversations into the

mix. You can read anything that interests both of you, or you can take turns reading books you each pick. You can also do this as a theme and go from there. Educational books can work well with this, too.

15. **Walk**- Go for a walk, hike, or take the dog out with your partner. You do not necessarily have to talk while you do this, but it can make a nice opportunity for doing so while being close and getting in some feel-good exercise. This can also be an effective tool for you to use if you find you need to think about a situation or calm down before discussing something with your partner. Fresh air and exercise can help you focus and ease your mind.

16. **Body language**- Be mindful of your body when you're talking to your partner. Are you closed off, have your arms crossed, or are you leaning away from them? This body language can convey that you don't want to talk to them, you're not going to be transparent, or that you aren't interested in or happy with their presence. It may not be what you are feeling, but as humans, we automatically read body language and gather clues from it. Your body language could look confrontational when you actually don't mean for it to. You can also use touch to show closeness and affection - a hand on the shoulder, a pat on the thigh, or the holding of hands.

Find What Works for You

When it comes down to it, your relationship is you and your partner's alone. What works for everyone else is a good starting point for you, but it may not be exactly what you need. Keep this discussion with your partner open. You can both come up with ways that you find work better for you than others. Most of the time, you do not know until you try. Be creative and keep an open mind. You're on a journey of discovery of yourself, of your partner, and of your relationship. If something doesn't work for you, don't give up hope, as there are a variety of other things you can try.

Reference the Enneagram when you find yourself void of ideas. There are many clues there as to what may work for some types that won't work for others. Remember to consider what you're feeling at the moment. If you're on the line of disintegration, you may find it harder to discover things that work effectively.

Chapter 10 : Common Misconceptions and Frequently Asked Questions

While there is no inherently wrong way to go about self-discovery, there are some common misconceptions about the Enneagram that are worth covering.

Relying Too Much on the Test

The tests for the Enneagram types is an excellent tool to help you along the way if you feel stuck. First and foremost, you should get acquainted with the type descriptions. See what jumps out at you the most. It's through the descriptions that many people are able to point out their type; this may be more obvious for some people than others. Consider the type descriptions that make the most sense in regards to your own personality and why. Is one of them making you feel defensive or is one of them making you feel like you could have written it about yourself? It's often one of those two that you will find your type in. The test itself is not the be all end all. It can be helpful if you find yourself left with too many choices. It's not uncommon for people to see a bit of themselves in multiple types. Some of this has to do with the disintegration and integration of the energy through the Enneagram in relation to the types. You also have your wing or subtype that you'll find yourself feeling connected to. Your instincts will serve you well here. Connecting with your personality type is the first step in self discovery that you usually make using the Enneagram. It is a very important step.

It Isn't Your Normal "Personality Test"

The Enneagram is a more in-depth holistic and spiritual approach to who we are as people than the typical personality test. The personality types have become the most popular aspect of the symbol, and the symbol itself is rooted in ancient teachings and filled with spiritually toned knowledge from many places in the world throughout our history. It's the modern day symbol that has brought the personality types to the forefront. Again, this is an excellent tool, but it goes deeper than your typical psychometric personality assignments. For example, the Myers-Briggs is a popular personality test today among many others. When talking about their results using the Myers-Briggs or similar tests, they may discuss them by stating that they're an ENTJ or other type without anymore thought to the matter. Those results were what people were after and all it offered them, whereas the Enneagram helps you dive deeper into your motivations, your fears, and your core, and it helps you along the road of self discovery, to name a few things.

Using Results as an Excuse

When discussing the Enneagram with other people, you may find that your first instinct is to discuss your results as you would another personality test by, for example, saying things like, "I'm a 3". When we do this (especially when you are first getting started), you are ignoring or discounting one of the integral parts of the Enneagram that it would not exist without: self-discovery. Often, people use their results to excuse their behavior, and they use those excuses to avoid changing, again negating the whole point of the Enneagram, which is self discovery. To be fair, you are welcome to use the Enneagram in any depth that you choose; however, when you ignore the bigger picture of the Enneagram, you are doing yourself and the people you discuss it with a disservice.

Typing Others

It is difficult to avoid typing other people around you once you learn about the different Enneagram types. You begin to get enthusiastic and excited, and you want to use the knowledge that you have in every way you can. Typing others may seem like a good idea at the time, and while it does not hurt to point out that somebody may be a specific type when introducing them to the idea of the Enneagram, you want to leave typing up to that individual. Typing itself is a very personal experience, so you should only do so for yourself.

Only Viewing One Aspect

Understandably, it's common for people to read their type and hyper focus on the negative aspects of it. There is something to be said for making note of them and working towards a healthier you, but when it's all you focus on, you are missing so much more. No one person is perfect, as we all have traits that can be seen as good, bad, or both. That's the nature of humans. We cannot necessarily get rid of our more negative traits, but we can learn to cope and be mindful of them. It's through using the Enneagram that you can help counter the traits that you discover affect you negatively.

Answering Questions

This may not be so much a misconception in the sense that people ask it but rather something that people end up doing without giving it much thought. You will get the most accurate answer when you are completely honest. By not thinking too much about each question and answering them by instinct, the first response you think to use is usually the most accurate. Some people will answer the questions in an idealistic manner based on the kind of person they would like to be. Using this method, you will likely not get an valid result.

Frequently Asked Questions about the Enneagram

1. How do I figure out what type I am if I score the same on more than one type?

First, read through each type description; the test is not always necessary to take. If you're stuck looking through the descriptions, you can take the test to help you out. If you then find that your score is the same for more than one of the types you were already considering, reread the descriptions. The answer often lies in the motivations behind each type. Some types are similar in certain ways, but the motivations for each one are what distinguish them from one other.

2. Can your type change? I feel like I am sometimes different types; is it possible to have more than one?

You have a base type that does not change, and you can have a subtype that you take on traits of. You also have traits that come from your line of integration and disintegration, which are also from other types. So, it's easy to find traits from other types in yourself, because at time you do embody them.

3. What do the lines inside the symbol mean?

The lines are the connections and flow of energy between the types. You can follow two of the lines coming from your type to see what your line of integration and disintegration are.

4. Do I need to seek out a teacher to learn the Enneagram?

No, you do not need to do this; it's not a rule of the Enneagram. There is a lot of information available in books and online these days. You will find that there are many teachers that you can turn to these days, as they have become quite popular, so if you decide to go down this route, you should have several at your disposal.

Real Life Problems Starting

Scott shares his early experience with the Enneagram. His story illuminates the importance of typing only yourself. He provides us with a great perspective on typing someone else and then sharing this with them.

I feel like I have done everything wrong when it comes to the Enneagram. That sounds like an oddly bold statement and maybe even a little self deprecating. It's true, though. When I was first told about the Enneagram, I only knew that it was a personality type. "I'm a definitely a seven and you're a six," I was told during the initial conversation. I was confused about what numbers had to do with who I am which is when I was told that it was a personality test. I looked it up later and took one of those free online tests. My results indicated I was a type nine. After reading the descriptions to see what I actually was, I decided I am a nine after all. I was a little annoyed that my friend had typed me and did it wrong, but I ended up getting caught up in the descriptions because of that. I wanted to know about them, too. Before I knew it, I was seeing types everywhere. I was typing my friends, teachers, and family; I even typed the mailman after a quick talk with him one evening. No one was safe from my psychometric prowess. I kept typing people, and telling them about it all the time. That is, until I tried to type a new friend of mine. I wasn't typing people out of anything malice; I was doing it to tell them about the Enneagram and how intriguing I had found it. I didn't know much about it, just very basic stuff, but I could see there was so much more to it, and I wanted to learn more. I hadn't bothered learning more by the time I was typing people. Anyway, this friend stopped me as soon as I mentioned that I was sure she was a three. She had taken a class the year before and was just as interested in the Enneagram as I was. She told me she wasn't a three, and that she is an eight, and then she explained why I shouldn't be typing people. I felt pretty bad about it, but in hindsight I just didn't realize it. It makes sense that you have to type yourself. I had initially been pretty annoyed when my other friend typed me incorrectly. Once my new friend realized I didn't know much about the Enneagram, she offered to tell me what she knew and encouraged me to ask any questions I had. It was then that I truly jumped in and started discovering myself using the Enneagram. I have learned so much about myself and what makes me work the way I do. I have been able to get my grades up and focus more, and I have stopped typing other people. I share my type with people now when I am talking about the Enneagram, and even though I do have suspicions about people's types, I keep those thought to myself. I have found that typing people has both helped and hindered me. With people I really know, most of them have taken the test and shared their results with me, so I have adjusted where I have needed to with them, and I have achieved some pretty good results. I definitely fight less with my family now. If I'm being honest, I've also had some luck using it in group projects without having everyone type themselves. I think it's best to let people type themselves now, but when you know something, it's hard not to just do it. I think one should try to maintain a balance between knowing that it's only a guess and knowing not to say anything about it.

Scott brings up some great points about typing other people. It's hard not to do this, and although we should try not to, many of us will still create guesses. Like with everything in life, it is all about balance. Someone who knows their partner, family member, or best friend very well may be able to accurately type them. The only problem is that you do not actually know for sure until you have them do it themselves.

Chapter 11 : Write it Out

Write hard and clear about what hurts. - Ernest Hemingway

Writing things down is one of the best tools you can use while learning. Physically writing something instead of using a device like a computer or tablet allows the brain to absorb it better. This is why you're more likely to retain information you have written down instead of something you have merely read. Taking notes is a well-known form of this practice in classrooms around the globe. How can you use writing to learn about the Enneagram and for self-discovery? You can do so by doing the same thing you would in a classroom, and that is taking notes on the information you're gathering and learning about. This will help you retain the information. Interestingly, it can also help you achieve any goals you set in regards to self-discovery.

Harvard did a study about setting goals and how they are fulfilled. Graduate students in the Harvard MBA program were asked about their goals for the future. If they had goals, were they clear and written, and did they have plans in place to carry them out to make them a reality? Of the students asked, 3 percent had written out goals with plans to carry them out, 13 percent had goals in mind but not written out, and 84 percent did not have any goals. 10 years later, the students were contacted again to see where they were now. The 13 percent of students that had goals in mind earned twice as much as the students with no goals. That 3 percent of students that had their goals written out and had plans in place for them earned around 10 times as much as the 97 percent of the combined class (Matthews, n.d.).

It's quite interesting to look at where you started and compare it to where you are now. Documenting your journey in self-discovery is one of several ways to do this; you should find out what works best for you. As a suggestion, writing is a good place to start. You can write about everything you're learning and discovering, asking yourself questions and creating goals. You can also use writing itself as a tool for self-discovery.

Writing in Your Relationship

Who doesn't love to get a handwritten letter? They're the paramount of romance in the media and hold an air of nostalgia with them these days. You can use writing to let your partner know you're thinking of them, to be romantic, and to spice things up a bit. In fact, it's something you should put on your to-do list as a surprise for your loved one.

Another way you can use writing within your relationship is to set goals. As a couple on a discovery journey together, it is worth not only documenting what you are doing, learning, and working on, but also working out issues that may arise. Even writing little notes to one another about a question you may have is an effective way to communicate clearly with your partner.

Handwritten letters may historically be romanticized, but they're also an interesting and effective tool for people who have trouble verbally expressing their thoughts and emotions. Writing out your thoughts and feelings about an issue for yourself can help you work through it. Writing it for your partner can allow you to get out what you might not verbally be able to at that moment. If you go this route, it's best to use "I statements". These are statements that allow you to talk about you and your feelings without placing blame on the other person, making them feel attacked as a result. When someone feels attacked, they get defensive and focus on that, leaving any more discussion on the matter hard to have, and the point gets missed. While it may not work every time, it's more likely to succeed this way.

As we already know from the Harvard study, it's a good idea to write down the goals you have. This is a good exercise for building your relationship. When you talk about and set goals together, you gain a clearer picture of what you both want and what you will be working towards. Also, when you write your goals down, you're more likely to accomplish them. Two people working towards a common goal allows each person support, and people usually do better with a good support system. Work on making this an effective tool in your relationship repertoire.

When you write down your goals or work through something with your partner, it is best to be mindful of perception. We experience things for ourselves and gain the knowledge and life experiences we do; this is how we form our perceptions. Our perception is how we view the world, situations, people, and other things. It's inherently flawed and is commonly the cause for arguments and confrontations between people. Your reality and your perception are not the same as someone else's, which can make resolving issues tricky. Everyone feels like they're right based on their perception. Stephen Covey covers this in his book, "The 7 Habits of Highly Effective People". In the book, he says relationships fail because of what we focus on. We focus on changing our superficial attitudes and behaviors in lieu of (or prior to) addressing the way we perceive the actual relationship itself (Covey, 2014). On top of that, you'll also find that your type can cause issues when trying to communicate clearly, and this is another reason why writing is an effective form of clear communication. Texting or emailing takes the personal aspect out of the act, so it's not suggested over physically writing for many of the same reasons that it's not as effective for studying.

7 Writing Activities

1. **Write out your type-** A great way to learn about your own and your partner's types is to write out their descriptions. Make notes, and ask yourself questions along the way. You can discuss your feelings about being this type, and try to ask yourself whether it's what you expected or if you're happy, disappointed, or indifferent about it. Your feelings are valid.

2. **Write out your individual goals-** Set goals for yourself in relation to self improvement and discovery. You're not only more likely to achieve them if you do so, but it also makes it more likely that they'll sink in, making you even more likely to work on them.

3. **Leave reminders around-** Speaking of goals, you can hand write notes and leave them in places to remind yourself and your partner. This is similar to the self-esteem boosting post-it note exercise. Place a sticky note on your mirror with a positive affirmation written on it. That way, every time you look in the mirror, you see something positive. This can also be used to help you achieve your goals and can be adapted for the goals you make in relation to self-discovery. For example, people who are trying to lose weight might place a note on the fridge to remind them to make a healthy choice. Another great use for sticky notes or just notes in general is to leave them for your partner. This is a sweet gesture that helps build on your relationship. You can leave notes with compliments, affirmations of love, etc.

4. **Journal-** Using a journal is an interesting and effective tool to not only keep track of what is going on with you, your life, your discoveries, and your spiritual self, but it's also a great place to find clues. Stream of consciousness writing is a useful way to go about this. When you're simply writing what comes to mind without prior thought, you are left with genuine and authentic writing. It's like reading your inner dialog - those thoughts in the back of your mind that you often are not even aware of.

5. **Work out problems-** Ernest Hemingway said it best when he proclaimed, "Write hard and clear about what hurts." If you find something is bothering you, such as a conflict or confrontation with your partner, you can both do this exercise. Write out what happened from your perspective on a piece of paper, using just the facts as you see them. On a separate piece of paper, write why it's bothering you to vent and let it out. Take a moment to breathe and compose yourself. On a third piece of paper, write a letter to your partner. Explain how you perceive the situation to be, how it made you feel (without the venting), and how you would like to go about resolving the issue.

6. **Compassion-** Self-compassion is an important part of self-improvement and a good tool in self-discovery. You can learn much about yourself when you try to access your compassionate self. Many of us feel that it's easy to be a compassionate person; it is being compassionate to oneself that is difficult for most. There are some self-compassion tests you can take to see the difference between your compassion for others and for yourself. The results are fascinating and normally very telling. In any case, everyone can use more self-compassion or learn how to exercise their self-compassion. When you can be compassionate to yourself as much as you would someone

else, you improve your mental health, in turn allowing you to grow and push farther. Write a letter to yourself about something you've been struggling with lately. Write it as if the person struggling is not you, and as though you are supporting a loved one. Then, read the letter back to yourself.

7. **Observe and track-** The Enneagram points to areas where we may have trouble, such as automatic behaviors or tendencies we have that are not helpful to us. Twos, for example, like to help people, even when it overrides their needs. You can track and keep yourself aware when these situation arise. By doing this and becoming more self-aware, you'll be able to combat it. You can physically write this down to track it, even if just adding it into your journal if you are deciding to use one everyday. Another thing that may be helpful to track with is a planner if you keep one.

Chapter 12 : Enneagram in All Your Relationships

Our entire life is filled with relationships, both good and bad, positive and negative, fulfilling and dissatisfying, and casual and intense. The older we get, the more we gain and the more experiences we have with them. We all know relationships and connections between people can be messy, confusing, and full of issues, but they do not have to be. Most of the relationships in your life can be saved if they're worth having in your life.

It's important to know the difference between a relationship that is worthwhile for you and one that is not. A worthwhile relationship is one that, even if it has some issues, is still a positive one and one that you want in your life. Putting your energy towards these kinds of relationships that have a great potential to be healthy relationships is an investment in your future and your own mental health. If you feel like you may need to let go of a relationship, no matter what kind it is, your instinct is often right in this situation. Some deep thought and introspection will help you determine this. Look to the Enneagram and check for some insights in your own type for situations like these. For example, if you're a nine, you may find that you're letting people do things to you or bring you down because you want to avoid confronting the negativity and conflict.

The Enneagram is a useful tool in all of your relationships, just as all aspects of your life benefit from self-discovery and self-improvement. It's worth considering the relationships in all areas of your life and not just your intimate ones.

The Enneagram at Work

The Enneagram has become a popular tool among businesses in recent years. Because the Enneagram is a particularly helpful tool for leadership development, emotional intelligence, and communication skills, it's used in businesses today to help with production, leadership, management, and peer relations.

If you're working a full-time job, you are likely spending a good 40 hours (give or take) with your co-workers every week. That's roughly 2,000 hours a year. That is a lot of time that you're spending with other people. Your time at work and your relationships with your co-workers should be positive considering this.

You can use the Enneagram at work in various ways, and you can use it in your more personal and friendly relationships with co-workers and perhaps with people you consider to be friends. Knowing their type can help resolve conflicts and aid in strengthening your relationship. When someone feels understood, it makes them feel good, it supports them, and it makes their relationship with the person who understands them a positive and stronger one.

If you are in a position at work where you watch over a group of people or happen to do a lot of group work, the Enneagram is an especially helpful tool. In fact, many companies already use personality tests to see what exactly they're working with and even when they're considering giving promotions. With a group of people that need to work closely together, it's beneficial to see how those people will interact. The Enneagram can also help you see where people's strengths and weaknesses are so assignments can be handed out accordingly for the most effective production.

Your Friends and Family

Your relationships with friends and family are important ones to nurture and pay attention to. Knowing your kids and relatives is a critical part of your success in these home based relationships. To improve on yourself in your roles as a parent, child, or sibling, it is beneficial to know what drives the people around you, such as what they desire and what their fears are. This is a particularly significant point. Just as we want to improve our romantic relationships, our familial relationships are similar and just as important.

While your kids need to be past early childhood to be appropriately typed, you can still use your observations to help them and improve on your parenting. Knowing what drives your child and what they're afraid of can give you a lot of insight into how they work and why. Their behavior is a particular place of interest here. Often, parents are confused by their children's behavior, especially if there's a more sudden change to it. There are obviously signs you still need to look out for and questions you still need to ask, but with some more basic issues, the Enneagram can be very helpful in situations like these. Tensions can run high in a home with children, and using the Enneagram to help resolve and limit conflict is a great place to start.

Speaking of tensions, many of us have certain family members that do not get along well, or maybe you do not get along very well with a few people. Family dynamics can be incredibly interesting, but they are even more interesting when you throw in personality types. Being able to navigate your relationships with your family members more easily can be a big help; knowing their types can help you see in what ways they are motivated and where those motivations are coming from. Also, when conflict does arise, it's a helpful tool in regaining the peace and working out the root causes.

Your family and those friends that are dearest to you are likely the most important people in your life. Therefore, it's vital to provide them with time, dedication, and energy. Your relationships can thrive, you can resolve or avoid conflict, and you can have happier and healthier relationships by digging deep and looking at people's motivations and what makes them tick.

Talk about your experiences with the Enneagram and what you're using it for with your friends and family. That will likely get people's attention enough to at least type themselves. If more people are on board, the more effective and easier it will become. By sharing your type with them, you are enabling them to do the same for you. When everyone is working towards a common goal, talking about it, and learning, the more effective everyone will be. In numbers come strength and support. Through the support of your loved ones, you'll be able to thrive as a family unit.

Real Life Family Enneagram

Below are a couple of stories about how the Enneagram helped two families. The first one is a story by Amelia. Hers is about her mother and aunt and what happened from her perspective when her mother decided to use the Enneagram to mend a relationship. The second story is from the perspective of a mother who was very unsure of herself. She felt inadequate and ill-equipped to be a parent, and she took those fears and turned them into knowledge. Jennifer's inspiring story about how she overcame her parenting fears and later used the Enneagram to help out her children is a prime example of how the Enneagram can be used in family life.

I have what I would consider a pretty typical family. We all love each other, but we don't always all get along, and this is a pretty typical family dynamic from what I have seen. My family has changed a lot since I was little. I've had a lot of people come in and out of it, so our dynamics have changed quite a bit, but even still, we have managed to keep a fairly normal relationship structure. My mom and my aunt in particular don't get along. They have found a lot of conflict throughout their lives together, even when they were kids. A lot of people like to blame it on the fact that they are the older and middle children, whereas the youngest of the family doesn't really have problems with anybody; middle child syndrome is what they call it. My mom and my aunt fight about everything. At one point, it got so bad that they couldn't even go to the same family functions. There wasn't actually much reason for them to be arguing all the time, except for that they just seem to clash with each other. We're talking about 45 years of fighting between these two people. Everyone just acted as though it was normal, and nobody ever expected it to stop. If anything, they expected it to just get worse over the years. And for a while, it did. The more they fought, the more grudges were held, and that made them fight even more; it just kept snowballing. A few years ago, I discovered the Enneagram, and I started on my self-discovery journey. I bought all the books I could and even went to a couple of workshops. My mom took notice of me being so interested in something. She had recently commented on how much my life has changed, and on how well I've been doing in contrast to my earlier years. I reminded her about her comment and explained to her that I've been using the Enneagram to help me, and through self-discovery, I was able to improve myself. I showed her the website with the types on them and told her she should read them. As soon as she was done, she asked me where she could take the test. So, I got her onto the website where she took the test, first asking her what she thought her type might be to begin with. She wasn't sure, so she took the test, and when she had finished and got her results, she wasn't all that surprised. It turns out that was the type that had jumped out to her to begin with, but she didn't want to say anything in case she wasn't right. I thought my mom's interest might stop when she knew her type, and for a little while, it did - or at least it looked that way to me. However, it turns out she had been reading on her own. I had recently broken up with my boyfriend, and my mom was comforting me by talking one night. She asked if I thought the Enneagram had anything to do with us breaking up or if it could have helped our relationship. And honestly, I had given it some thought myself already. I had tried using it some to help improve our relationship, but the relationship just wasn't right for me, so I decided to let it go. I told my mom that relationships could be improved with the Enneagram and that working on yourself can improve your relationships. The next day my mom asked to borrow a couple of angiogram books, and I obliged. By the time Thanksgiving rolled around, my mom reached out to my aunt and invited her over to our house for dinner. This is something that was unheard of at the time. They hadn't had a family meal together in at least a couple of years. Our family usually splits up holidays between different families or we would meet up at different times. My mom and my aunt always worked around this so that they wouldn't see each other. So, my mom inviting my aunt over was shocking. I asked her why she did, as this just wasn't normal anymore. My mom replied that she had been working on herself for months now and that she had taken the time to think about what I had said about my relationship and how improving myself could improve others. She had given it a lot of thought; she didn't like where her relationship was with her sister, and she wanted to make it better. So, she decided to give it a shot. That Thanksgiving, my aunt came over, and we had a lovely dinner together. There were some moments of tension where I thought everything was going to crumble, but my mom held it together. My aunt even ended up staying after dinner that night, and my mom showed her the Enneagram. My aunt took the test as well. When my aunt's results were revealed, they both laughed. It turns out my mom and my aunt are both eights. My aunt didn't go far with her Enneagram journey, but my mom and my aunt now go to the same family meals together, they celebrate birthdays and holidays, and they even talk on the phone sometimes. I can't say that they don't argue still and that there aren't some problems that persist, but my mom and my aunt gave new life to a relationship that had been bad for most of their lives. Because of my mom's work and self-improvement, she made that happen and I couldn't be prouder.

Even in the healthiest families conflict, arises; that's human nature. Amelia's touching story of her family overcoming a bad relationship using the Enneagram is a touching one. It's also a good lesson to all of us and an excellent example of the power of ourselves.

When I found out I was pregnant, I was terrified. I didn't have a very good childhood, and my parents weren't great parents to me. In fact, for most my life, they weren't parents at all. The moment I found out I was pregnant, I realized I didn't know how to be a parent. The closer it got to my due date, the more worried I was. When my son was born, I looked into his eyes, and I knew I wanted to do better; I knew I wanted to be a good parent. There is no love like a mother for her child. Because I didn't have a great relationship with my parents, I didn't feel equipped to be a parent, and once my son was born, I decided that was going to change. I started reading all the parenting books I could to learn every bit of information I could possibly get my hands on. As my son got older and our family grew, I realized I had made it quite far. I had done that by working on myself. When I started having some trouble with my son's behavior, I sought help online. Someone suggested to me that I type him using the Enneagram. So I went and looked it up and started reading about it; I figured I would try anything at this point. I read the descriptions, and I thought I figured out what he was, but I wanted to know for sure. He was 15 at this point, so it seemed like a good time to type him. It turns out that my amazingly creative 15-year-old son is a type 4, and that fits him perfectly. Finding out my son's type and seeing how perfectly it fit him, I started taking more notice to what he was saying and doing, and realized he must be feeling very down. He was withdrawn and moody, and for a while I had chalked it up to him just being a teenager. I'm sure a lot of it is, but I still wanted to be a better parent. I wanted to help him in any way I could, even if he was just being a teenager. I decided to type myself and my husband and we both felt that ours was pretty spot-on as well. I decided to give the Enneagram a decent shot, just how I had when my not-so-little one was indeed little. I tested my theory and information I had gained by giving him some space and letting him know I was there to talk if he needed it. My son is normally a very creative person, but he didn't really have any hobbies. I thought it would benefit him to have a way to express himself, so I took him to the art store and told him to pick some supplies out. At first, he thought I was a little crazy, but was happy to have the opportunity to buy something. He ended up getting a sketchbook, some pencils, an eraser, some markers, watercolor paint, and a little pad of paper. Once we were done, I took him out for a quick bite to eat and explain why I took him to the store to buy these things. I told him I thought he could use an opportunity to express himself and that I was still there if he needed to talk. That evening, he spent the entire night in his room. I woke up to a lovely handwritten note in the morning that was left by my 15-year-old son, along with a beautifully painted picture of my favorite flower. In the note, my moody teenage son took the time to pour his heart out to me and thank me. It was one of my better parenting moments, and one I'll never forget. To this day, my son still draws and paints to express himself through art. He began opening up to me more after that day to work through some of the problems he was having. It turns out that he's a pretty sensitive guy. Now that my daughter is old enough, I've typed her, as well, and she's a 3 just like her dad.

Jennifer's story about her family is an interesting one. Inspired by her fears, she used her children as motivation for self-improvement, and it worked out very well for her. Jennifer has used the Enneagram to help her connect with her children, so this is a great example of what the Enneagram can do. She's the type to get a little more insight into her son's motivations and what might help him out. It turns out she was right and engaged him in a lifelong healthy way to cope with his feelings and emotions with a hobby that increases skill and emotional intelligence. The Enneagram works very well with parenting for many of these reasons. You needn't only use it for your children, but also for yourself to find out where you may be lacking in your parenting skills or what might be happening in your personal life that affects your abilities to be a parent. You'll also find that the better your relationship is with your spouse, the better and healthier your family life is in general, and that also has a positive effect on your children.

Bonus Chapter: "Enneagram Self Discovery"

The Enneagram Wings

There is a lot more to the Enneagram than the 9 personality types that were covered over the last 9 chapters. The personalities are just one aspect of the model, and chances are after you had read about the personality types, you had wondered if anyone really has personalities that are so extreme which were described in each of the chapters. The odds of that being the case are low because even though the personality types are what people's cores are like, they are usually watered down or influenced by other personality types.

The reasons that the personality types are colored or are influenced are because part of the Enneagram model consists of wings, which are responsible for altering the personality types as it is referenced in the late Riso's book, *Personality Types: Using the Enneagram for Self-Discovery*.

If you remember back earlier in the eBook that the personality types were compared to having a plain flavored vanilla ice cream, that in itself seems bare. The same goes for personality types. However, what you need to change it up and to flavor, it is to add toppings which could be fudge sauce, caramel sauce, or sprinkles, or nuts, whatever you choose, that is what makes the ice cream sundae more complete. The ice cream or sundae toppings are what the wings of the Enneagram model represent. The spice that is added to the core in order to make the individual more complete.

In other words, the wings are the neighboring personality types that are right next to the core type on the Enneagram model. These wings do influence your core, but they do not alter your core type just like the sundae toppings do not change the fact that the type of ice cream that they are laid over is the vanilla ice cream.

Here is a better analogy to make this clearer. Our core type is our personality type. That represents the vanilla ice cream, but if you put fudge sauce over it, then that represents the influence of one neighboring wing type. And if you put sprinkles on it, then that represents the other neighboring wing's influence on the other side.

However, in some cases, both wings are highly influential, and in other cases, one wing is more influential than the other, and that all depends on the circumstance that the individual is in. These wings are helpful and can be resourceful, and they are also there to help balance the individual as well.

Think back again to the airplane analogy. An airplane needs its wings in order to stay balanced in the air. The core by itself will not be able to do that job. The wings help keep the individual balanced as the core type by itself would not be able to maintain that type of balance at all.

The purpose of the wings is to help bring a new perspective to an individual when they are faced in any type of challenging or any type of situation. The wings also are beneficial when it comes to emotions and behavior. Let's take a look at some examples of how the wings can be beneficial to each of the 9 personalities on the Enneagram model in the next section as it will start from Type 1 to Type 4.

Type One To Type Four And Their Wings

In this section, you will learn about the first 4 types of personalities and how their types are altered by their wings when necessary:

Type 1 - The Perfectionist - The perfectionist only wants perfection and cannot stand anything that is less than perfect. The main fear that the One has is that he or she is afraid of being corrupt in any way and wants to be balanced and have integrity. The wings will help create more balance for the Ones. The Type One with a Nine wing would have influences from the Nine personality type and would provide them with a calmer approach. They still have their strong expectations, but they will be able to allow things to unfold when they rely on the Nine wing.

The Type One with a Two wing will be more of an advocate. They want perfection, and they want to help make a situation better. If a Type One goes into a homeless shelter and sees that there is abuse going on, and wants to improve things for the situation, then the One will lean on to the Two wing to advocate for the safety and better treatment of the individuals.

Type 2 - The Helper - The helper wants to please others and be there for others but has a strong possessive side. However, if Type Two relies on the One wing, then that shapes the individual for being more of a servant to others. That does not literally mean they will be maids or butlers. However, they will be the ones to deliver messages to others to make sure it is delivered properly.

Type Two with a Three wing will be the type to host events or to teach others what they have learned that can be helpful. They still want to be appreciated, and that is why those with this personality type who learn on Wing Three will be the ones to hold events or to go and teach in settings that they know that they will get their kudos for putting themselves out there.

Type 3 - The Performer - The performer is naturally charming and is only concerned about being ambitious for the sake of being the best at what they do. And they want to beat their competition as well. And, in order for them to win others over, even more, they will rely on their Two Wing in order to help others which means that they will gain what they need.

This sounds like they are strictly taking advantage of people in order for them to win, but when they rely on their Two Wing, they will genuinely help someone who is in need, but they do need to get something back from it. When the Three leans on the Four Wing, they tap into their unique side and turn it into something professional. Type Threes that are entrepreneurs have to lean towards the Four Wing in order to differentiate themselves from the competition.

Type 4 -The Romantic - This individualistic type is always looking for ways to seek out their identity because of how they fear that they have no real significance. They are quite melodramatic as well. However, the Fours that lean on their Three Wing can be unique yet have an approach to go after something which will give them confidence that they have a purpose to fulfill.

The Four that leans on the Five Wing will be more like a Bohemian, as they will realize that they are unique and will embrace it without having to make their mark. They will not throw their uniqueness in people's faces and will find a way to live comfortably with who they are on their own.

The next and final section of this chapter will focus on Type 5 to Type 9 personalities and its wings.

Type Five To Type Nine And Their Wings

In the late Riso's book, *Personality Types: Using the Enneagram for Self-Discovery* plenty of information about the personality types and their wings on the Enneagram model are covered. In the previous section, the brief descriptions of the Type One to Type Four personalities and their wings were covered. In this section, the Type Five to Type Nine personality types and their wings will be focused on before going into the next chapter which is going to be about the Enneagram centers.

However, before that is covered, let's finish this chapter by covering the wings for the Type Five to Type Nine personality types on the Enneagram model.

Type 5 - The Investigator - As you know that the Fives are quite secluded, and secretive, and they are the observers, and they spend their time gathering up information. They are not the type to make friends easily unless they find someone who they relate to and can become friends for life. In fact, their main fear is that they may end up useless and incapable. And their greatest yearning is that they are competent.

However, when the Investigator leans on the Four Wing, they become more of an iconoclastic type. They are the types that are ready to break traditions and are extremely bold thinkers. They are not afraid to rebel, and that is how they can work through their insecurities if necessary. For instance, the Five that is appalled by how a cult is brainwashing a group of people because the Five has already done research of their own to see how damaging they are can easily lean on the Four Wing in order to make a bold move by exposing the type of damage the cult has caused with proof. That will most definitely make people wake up, especially the ones who have been affected.

The Fives that learn on the other wing, which is the Six Wing end up becoming problem-solvers. The Fives are distrusting like the Sixes are, however, the Sixes are the ones that yearn to find someone or something to trust which is the biggest challenge for the Six. If the Five comes across something or someone that they are attracted to, then they can learn towards their Six Wing in order to determine how trustworthy someone is, or whether getting involved in something they are interested in is worth it. They will evaluate whether the individual or situation deserves a chance through critical thinking.

Type 6 - The Loyalist - The Loyalist is always distrusting and yearns to find something or someone to trust. They want to be committed to something or to someone and need security. However, even though they are responsible and engaging, they are extremely anxiety-ridden and suspicious. They are terrified without having support or proper guidance, and their main desire is to have the support they need as well as the security as they do not like going out of their comfort zones.

The Type Six with a Five-Wing are the types to defend others if they know they are innocent in a situation or understand their situation as to why they did something that may be unpopular. For instance, if a worn-out parent had no choice but to put their disabled child into a group home and he or she received nothing but judgment and criticism for it, then the Loyalist leaning on the Five Wing would stand up and defend the parent. Even though the Loyalist would not understand on a personal level why the parent did what he or she needed to do, the Six would understand that the parent was burned out and could not help the child and would not hesitate to point that out to those who are judging the parent.

The Six leaning on a Seven Wing would be the type to leave their comfort zone a little and put their distrusting trait aside if they saw someone who was distraught. And, in this case, the Six would sit down next to the individual to listen to why he or she is quite upset just to give that person an ear. The Sixes are all about needing comfort and the Seven breaks the comfort zone, and in this case, the Seven Wing would help break that.

Type 7 - The Enthusiast - Sevens are adventure seekers and are naturally positive. They need to constantly have their needs fulfilled as to why they are always looking forward to the next best thing, and they are terrified of being deprived. The Sevens are not empathetic, but the Sixes are, and when the Sevens lean on their Six Wing, they want to make others happy who are having a rough time. That is why they are referred to as the entertainers, as they can easily cheer someone up who is having a bad day.

The Sevens are also not naturally practical or organized; however, their neighboring personality type the Eight is both powerful and practical. And when the Seven realizes that he or she has to be grounded to attain a goal, then this is when he or she leans on the Eight Wing and is just as powerful but is more realistic and organized about attaining a certain goal.

Type 8 - The Challenger - Type Eight is the bold, dominating, and confident type, and will never back down if a challenge is being faced. Those who have this personality type will not back down and are the ones who must always be in charge. Their biggest yearning is that they are always in charge no matter what, and that applies to life circumstances. They are deeply afraid of being controlled or harmed by others.

However, the Eights need to lean on their wings when it comes to certain situations. And the Eight has to realize at times that he or she cannot control life's circumstances and the only way that the Eight can find acceptance is by leaning on the Seven Wing. This causes the Eight to become innovative and creative by finding a solution to be in charge of an outside circumstance that cannot be changed.

For instance, if an Eight was on a ship that was about to

sink, he or she would jump off and swim over to a foreign island where he or she would not know anything about which includes the language. The Eight would find a way to learn a language and find temporary work to stay there until he or she could find a way to get back home or to the destination where he or she was heading.

And, for the Eight that needed to be in a position to protect someone else's needs, then they would lean on the Nine Wing for not just being the protector but being empathetic towards the one who needed protection. The Eight would lean on the Nine Wing to be concerned about someone else's needs other than their own if there was a situation that came up. For instance, the Eight could find a homeless individual who had been bullied. This would trigger the empathetic side in the Eight, and the Eight would then fight off the bully to help the homeless individual, and then even go and buy them a meal. That would be the result of them leaning on the Nine Wing.

Type 9 - The Peacemaker - This personality type is naturally empathetic, loyal, receptive, agreeing, complacent, and easygoing. They only want to have peace of mind, and their biggest fear is experiencing a loss. The Nine needs to lean on the Eight or One Wings in order to be in better control of their situations as well as the situations of those who they care for because without either of these wings, they will not survive with this personality type alone.

Nines that lean on the Eight Wing are referred to as the advocates. They are naturally empathetic; however, in some situations they need to be in better control of themselves or of others that are close to them. If they are in a situation where they are not getting the medical help they need for an illness they suspect they have, then they would need to lean on the Eight Wing and become bold and become their own advocates in order to receive better medical care. Or if their children were struggling in school and the teachers were not concerned, then they would be an advocate for their children to make sure that they get the type of help or education they are entitled to get. In other words, when push comes to shove, the Nine will need to rely on the Eight Wing.

And, the Nine will need to rely on the One Wing in order to turn their dream into a reality. Nines by themselves are not grounded. However, they have the ability to be, and that is when they can lean on the One Wing. The One Wing will help gain the skills and knowledge to turn their dream into something that really comes to live instead of just staying as a fantasy.

For instance, if the Nine wanted to become an author and even become a best-seller, then the Nine would investigate what could be done to make that happen by leaning on their Perfectionist Wing.

And that concludes the Wings of the Personality Types Of The Enneagram. The examination of the Enneagram model is not finished as the next chapter will be covering the centers which are also covered in the late Riso's book, *Personality Types: Using the Enneagram for Self-Discovery.*

Bonus Chapter: "Enneagram Self Discovery"

Introduction To Centers

The onion of the Enneagram has been peeled a lot as you had already discovered it's 9 personality types, and then after learning about those, you had learned about how the personalities are tempered by their wings. And now, you are going to be learning about the centers in the Enneagram model. All of the information about the centers are derived from the late Riso's book, Personality Types: Using the Enneagram for Self-Discovery.

The 9 personality types of the Enneagram model are placed into the 3 groups which are called the centers. Each center represents the imbalances that are found in each of the personality type, which is where the negative traits of each one happens to lie. The 3 centers are the Instinctive center, the Feeling center, and the Thinking center. And each center contains the 3 personality types that share the strengths and weaknesses of that center.

Each type of personality is affected by the unconscious emotional response to not being in contact with the core in the centers. That is why the centers have negative themes. The themes of the centers are:

- **The Instinctive Center** as the One, the Nine, and the Eight personality types fall into this area, and this area represents rage and anger

- **The Feeling Center** as the Two, the Three, and the Four personality types also fall into this center, and this area represents shame

- **The Thinking Center** as the Five, the Six, the Seven personality types falls into this area as well, and this center represents fear.

After reading about the personality types more in detail, then it is not difficult to understand how these personality types could end up falling into the centers that best represent their traits. The first center that will be examined more is the Instinctive center, and the One, the Nine and the Eight personalities will be examined further as to how they are affected by the centers.

The Instinctive Center

The Instinctive center is represented by anger and rage, and it is easy to see how the Eights can be full of anger and rage but may be more difficult to understand how the Nines and the Ones are affected. Let's look further into each of the personalities that fall into this center more carefully.

The Eights affected by the Instinctive center - The Eights are all about needing to be in control, and the anger they have is instinctive, and it builds which is what strengthens their motivations. However, even with the positive side to the anger in this personality type which is put to good use. If they feel as if they are about to lose control, then rage sets in. Their rage setting in is the response to them feeling threatened by a person or a situation that could potentially have control over them.

This results in rage which causes them to easily express violence. The Eights respond to their anger in a physical way which includes them being physically violent as well as them raising their voices. Their natural, confident nature is what gives them permission to express anger in this manner. However, the Nines are fueled by anger as well as they express it differently based on their personality type.

The Nines affected by the Instinctive center - The Nines are in the same center as the Eights, and this may be difficult to believe since they are opposites personality wise. But they are equally effectively by anger and rage based on the fact that they lie in the Instinctive Center.

However, whereas the Eights embrace their anger, the Nines do not as they deny it even though they are aware it is there.

The Nines shove it away as they are not in touch with this part of them in addition to their other instincts. Nines prefer to stick to their idealizations of the world. but if they are pushed, then that anger either comes bubbling up in an explosive manner or ends up affecting them by causing them to express their anger in a passive-aggressive way. The Nines avoid their anger, and the Ones also do not embrace and express their anger the same way as the Eights do, but in a different way.

The Ones affected by the Instinctive center - The Ones are all about perfection, and if they acknowledge their angry part, they feel as if they are less than perfect which is their ultimate nightmare. This is why the Ones do what they can do repress this side to them. They do not want to ever want to be seen as angry. However, as much as they want to deny the anger, they can't. The way they channel this instinctive anger is by directing towards their inner-critic and are also quite critical of others in a way that can sting. The Eights express this anger in a violent and visible way, the Nines do to not acknowledge it, but it comes bubbling up through an explosive temper that is momentary or causes them to become passive-aggressive, and the Ones express this anger by being overly and unfairly critical of themselves and of others.

That concludes the way the Instinctive center effects personality types One, Nine, and Eight of the Enneagram model. The next center to examine is the feeling center.

The Feeling Center

The Feeling center is governed by the feeling of shame which affects personality types Two, Three, and Four. The first one to be examined is how the Twos are affected by this center.

The Twos affected by the Feeling center - The Twos are well aware of their feelings of shame and the way they suppress it is by focusing heavily on how they can be liked by others. And as long as they feel that they are appreciated, they can focus on the positive feelings they have while suppressing any feelings of shame that they may be having. And the way they want people to like them and appreciate them in a desperate way is by helping others, and this even means they would be putting their own wants and needs aside just to suppress their feelings of shame.

And, when they are threatened by someone who doesn't

like them or if they do not feel appreciated, they are exposed to that shame, and this actually causes them to become angry. Their personality type is not in the Instinctive center, but shame also can bring up angry emotions which is why they are constantly feeling hysterical when they are not feeling appreciated for their efforts. The Threes also are doing what they can to suppress their feelings of shame in a different manner.

The Threes affected by the Feeling center - The Threes want to prove to themselves and to everyone else that they are winners in everything they do. They want to be the best at what is most important to them whether it is financial success or having the best-fit body. And they are constantly attempting to become the best in order to shove those uncomfortable feelings of shame which is why they are terrified of failure and feeling like they are adequate. Their extreme desire to be the best at what they do is so that they suppress their inner feelings of shame.

The positive attribute of this personality type is that this type is naturally driven even though it is for the wrong reasons. The Fours are governed by the Feeling center as well but in a much different way than the Twos and the Threes.

The Fours affected by the Feeling center - The

Threes do what they can do avoid feelings of inadequacy whereas the Fours are most likely to succumb to those feelings of shame instead. However, what the Fours do in order to hide those feelings is that they show off their creativity, proudly show off their eccentricities, and make their mark about being unique as well.

Fours also are affected by feelings of shame by creating a fantasy life which causes them to escape from them having to deal with anything uncomfortable that life continuously throws at them. They do this to not only escape anything that can cause them hardships, but they do this by escaping anything that does not interest them in the least bit.

That concludes the personalities affected by the Feeling center. The last center that will be focused on is the Thinking center which effects the Five, the Six and the Seven personality types.

The Thinking Center

The Thinking center is governed by fear and the Five, the Six and the Sevens are the personalities that fall into this center, which is easily seen after learning about the nature of these personality types. The first one to be covered is how the Fives are affected.

The Fives affected by the Thinking center - The one thing that the Fives fear the most is the external world. This is why they withdraw, are secretive and are observant, and learn what they can. They create their own inner worlds and will only allow those in it who they feel are not a threat in any way at all. Fives are seen as hermits because that is what they literally are in order to escape the outer world by keeping themselves within. They don't feel confident enough to join into the outer world, and this is based on their fear, which is why they keep to themselves.

The Sixes affected by the Thinking center - This personality type is affected by this center the most as they display plenty of anxiety over distrusting situations and people. And yet they have a strong desire to trust and have faith in others and in situations. Their fear is what prevents them from putting their distrusting and skeptical sides aside. They always find reasons to not trust someone or something even if there has been proof indicating that the individual or situation is completely Kosher.

And, Sixes will even doubt those who they have allowed them into their lives due to the fact that their fear is keeping them from being open and trusting in any way or form. They will also deal with their fear by being confrontational towards those who they do not trust which is driven by their anxiety over any situation that is causing them to be doubtful in the first place.

The Sevens affected by the Thinking center - The Fives fear the external world whereas the Sevens fear the internal world and their fear is the reason that the Sevens are constantly looking for excitement through external sources. This is the one personality type that will not be introspective in any way or form because they have to constantly look for excitement and adventure in order to escape the one thing they fear the most - and that is the inner world.

With that said, Sevens are not purposely shallow by them wanting to keep taking expensive trips and are obsessed with meeting celebrities, famous people, and people who they find to be worthy. The Sevens are not non-appreciative about the fact that they just went on an expensive trip and are looking forward to the next one each and every time. They are not purposely being thankless and taking their blessings for granted that most people would not have a chance to take even once in their lifetimes. The Sevens behave this way because they are absolutely terrified of being in their inner world and they are terrified of being trapped in it. They keep themselves engaged, busy, and occupied in many different activities at once just to escape their inner world.

That means the next time you think that someone who may be shallow for going on expensive trips all the time and not appearing to be thankful for their experiences may not be any of that at all. They may just be one of those Sevens that constantly need to escape due to the fact that they are driven by fear of being trapped. Their fear stops them from sitting down, breathing, and to smell the roses.

Conclusion

I can teach anybody how to get what they want out of life. The problem is that I can't find anybody who can tell me what they want. – Mark Twain

The journey you take with self-discovery is your own. It can take motivation and discipline, especially when you start coming across things you may not be so comfortable with; in those moments, it's easy to quit, but they are also the moments when you will do the most work on yourself. You'll take them head on and make it to the other side wiser and feeling more capable. This is when you'll find your voice and strength, which have always been there hiding. Tap into this and keep going.

Through discovering yourself, you'll find what you need and want within and outside of your life. You'll know instead of guess, and you will set goals and work towards them. You'll find yourself over and over again. The more you dig in, the more there is to discover. This is not overwhelming, but rather, it is enlightening. Remember that you and your life are worth the work it takes to learn and grow.

As you learn more about yourself, you will set your goals and work towards them; remember that writing them down will help you achieve them. You can dive as deep as you want into the Enneagram and into self discovery, but the techniques you've learned can undoubtedly aid you in all areas of your life.

Whatever type you are, remember to avoid focusing on the negative. Every type has both positive and negative traits. That's the truth for everyone - no exceptions. That doesn't mean you can't work towards being a healthier you. There's always room for improvement, as there's always something that can be worked on.

It's with yourself that your changes are made, and those changes impact the rest of your life and your reality. The more positive changes you make, the more positivity you will have in your life. The more you learn about yourself, the better you are able to navigate life and certain situations, and the more you self-improve, the more you will thrive. It is amazing how much allowing yourself to grow helps strengthen your relationships and everything else around you. We attract what we send out.

The most important thing you can do in your relationship aside from working on yourself individually is working together. Without each other, there is no relationship.

Communication and quality time is integral in learning about each other, about your relationship, and about what your goals are so you can grow and improve together.

All the relationships in your life can benefit from using the Enneagram. Just as all aspects of your life benefit from self-discovery and self-improvement, it's worth it to consider your relationships in all areas of your life and not only your intimate ones.

No matter your types and whether they look incompatible on paper or like they are puzzle pieces that fit together, they aren't worth trying to fix just because of type. There are no hard and set rules about who can get along with whom. Although, you may find that some people get along with others with less effort; such is life.

Whether you were attracted to this book because your relationship needs help, you and your partner were looking for something to do together, or you just like the Enneagram and wanted to utilize it in your relationship, I wish you well on your journey.

References

Beeson, L. (2016). Study challenges theory that good communication leads to marital satisfaction - UGA Today. Retrieved from https://news.uga.edu/good-communication-marital-satisfaction-0716/

Breines, J. (2016). Why You Have to Love Yourself First. Retrieved from https://www.psychologytoday.com/us/blog/in-love-and-war/201601/why-you-have-love-yourself-first

Covey, S. (2014). The 7 habits of highly effective people. New York: Simon & Schuster.

Deitz, B. (2016). 21 Ways Anyone Can Be A Better Partner. Retrieved from https://www.bustle.com/articles/150863-21-ways-anyone-can-be-a-better-partner

Enneagram Relationships - Do Opposites Attract? | 9types. Retrieved from http://www.9types.com/writeup/enneagram_relationships.php

How To Change Your Life Using The Enneagram — Part 2: Discover Your Type. (2016). Retrieved from https://medium.com/@BaysideChurch/how-to-change-your-life-using-the-enneagram-part-2-discover-your-type-e78fcdd396c

LaBier, D. (2016). Good Communication Alone Doesn't Improve Relationships. Retrieved from https://www.psychologytoday.com/us/blog/the-new-resilience/201610/good-communication-alone-doesnt-improve-relationships

Matthews, G. Retrieved from https://www.dominican.edu/academics/lae/undergraduate-programs/psych/faculty/assets-gail-matthews/researchsummary2.pdf

Merenda, P. (1987). Toward a Four-Factor Theory of Temperament and/or Personality. Journal Of Personality Assessment, 51(3), 367-374. doi: 10.1207/s15327752jpa5103_4

O'Hanrahan, P. Moving on the Lines — THE ENNEAGRAM AT WORK. Retrieved from https://theenneagramatwork.com/moving-on-the-lines

Orbuch, T. (2015). 5 simple steps to take your marriage from good to great.

Riso, D., & Hudson, R. (1996). Personality types. Boston: Houghton Mifflin.

Seppala, E. (2014). The Scientific Benefits of Self-Compassion - The Center for Compassion and Altruism Research and Education. Retrieved from http://ccare.stanford.edu/uncategorized/the-scientific-benefits-of-self-compassion-infographic/

Tartakovsky, M. (2018). 3 Tips for Bringing Out the Best in Your Relationship. Retrieved from https://psychcentral.com/blog/3-tips-for-bringing-out-the-best-in-your-relationship/

Traditional Enneagram (History) — The Enneagram Institute. (n.d.). Retrieved from https://www.enneagraminstitute.com/the-traditional-enneagram

Type Descriptions — The Enneagram Institute. Retrieved from https://www.enneagraminstitute.com/type-descriptions